ENGLISH LANGUAGE, LITERATURE
AND CREATIVE WRITING

ENGLISH LANGUAGE, LITERATURE AND CREATIVE WRITING

A Practical Guide for Students

Sarah Dobbs (ed.),
Val Jessop,
Devon Campbell-Hall,
Terry McDonough
and Cath Nichols

ANTHEM PRESS
LONDON · NEW YORK · DELHI

Anthem Press
An imprint of Wimbledon Publishing Company
www.anthempress.com

This edition first published in UK and USA 2014
by ANTHEM PRESS
75–76 Blackfriars Road, London SE1 8HA, UK
or PO Box 9779, London SW19 7ZG, UK
and
244 Madison Ave #116, New York, NY 10016, USA

British Library Cataloguing-in-Publication Data
A catalogue record for this book is available from the British Library.

Library of Congress Cataloging-in-Publication Data
English language, literature and creative writing : a practical guide for students / Dr Sarah
Dobbs (ed.), Dr Devon Campbell-Hall, Dr Val Jessop, Dr Cath Nichols, Terry McDonough.
pages cm
Includes bibliographical references and index.
ISBN 978-1-78308-288-9 (papercover : alk. paper)
1. English language–Rhetoric–Study and teaching. 2. Creative writing–Study and
teaching. I. Dobbs, Sarah, 1980– editor.
PE1404.E67 2014
808'.042071–dc23
2014024039

Cover image: Olga Danylenko/Shutterstock.com

ISBN-13: 978 1 78308 288 9 (Pbk)
ISBN-10: 1 78308 288 7 (Pbk)

This title is also available as an ebook.

CONTENTS

INTRODUCTION

This guide was born out of a genuine desire to help students. All of the authors of this book went into teaching in order to translate our knowledge and passion for our respective disciplines to others. Education can change lives. It has certainly changed ours and we genuinely want students to do as well as they can. When I was studying for my own English literature degree, I noticed the importance of understanding the impact of a particular module's learning outcomes. Looking at past exam papers, I started to make an educated guess at what future exam questions might look like. This helped organise my revision. There's no magic formula to getting the mark you want, but with a little common sense and our insight, we believe you'll be well on the way to achieving the degree you're hoping for. Some inside tips, as well applying a little logical thinking, can go a very long way – as well as saving you some precious time! We've included examples and analyses of student work, tasks that will help get you thinking in a way that will aid your study, and advice from previous students.

The 'golden' years of getting grants and easy funding to go to university is a thing of the past. We recognize that it's quite likely you're working in paid employment and taking care of your family. All this while trying to commit to one of the most intense – and inspirational – periods of your life. There are many wonderful textbooks that will provide you with in-depth explorations of, say, the evolution of English literature, or how to apply postcolonial theory. This book was written to help you pass your degree. Increasing your knowledge and stretching your own abilities will undoubtedly change your life. Whatever combination of English language, literature or creative writing that you're studying, we truly hope this book will help you on your way. But why study for a degree in these subjects? Are you still deciding which degree to do or what combination? I wanted to include Dr Devon Campbell-Hall's thoughts on the interconnection between English language, English literature and creative writing to help with this, but also to remind us of why we're interested in these disciplines in the first place. The best of luck in your academic career!

Sarah Dobbs

English Literature versus English Language versus Creative Writing

The variation between English degree courses is enormous – students can focus entirely on English language, English literature, creative writing, or a combination of these. Despite their main area of focus, most English degrees will include aspects of each of these disciplines. Professor Andrew Melrose argues: 'Creative writing students [...] have to be encouraged to read better, to read critically before they can think about writing what they read – and this is the legacy of critical theory as a writer's tool. [...] Thus the phrase: better readers make better thinkers make better writers'.[1]

To be a good writer, then, one must become a more effective critical reader, and to become a more effective reader, one must become a better critical and creative writer. In order to study the peculiarities of English linguistics (that is, the study of the English language and how it has developed and changed over the centuries), literature provides a rich source of examples of the wonderful quirks of our language. In order to understand the intricacies and beauty of English literature, it is helpful to have at least a basic grasp of linguistic analytical theories and concepts. To be an effective creative writer, elements of both of these are helpful.

If your degree is English language, you are likely to focus on linguistic theories, using literature as a source of examples of how the English language has changed through history. If your degree is in English literature, you will also analyse the power of language, but will spend the majority of your time deeply involved in literary texts as cultural artefacts which reflect the societies in which they were created and disseminated. However, some English degrees will include elements of language and literature, as well as a significant focus on creative and critical writing. This approach – which combines the traditionally academic with the practical – enables a deeper understanding of how successfully to decode and interpret texts created by others. One of my Making and Reading Poetry

---

1   Andrew Melrose, 'Reading and Righting: Carrying on the "Creative Writing Theory" Debate', *International Journal for the Practice and Theory of Creative Writing* 4, no. 2 (2007): 109–17 (113).

students wrote the following on their anonymous unit evaluation: 'Getting us to write poetry as well as read it was a stroke of genius! We were forced to try out the theories we had been studying at a safe distance, and this made us realise that these ideas were not just abstract, but practical. Through learning the how, we began to make sense of the why.'

Because the discipline of successfully completing an English degree signifies that students have not only learned to read and write both critically and creatively, successful graduates enter the employment market with a toolbox of exceedingly useful skills. An English degree shows potential employers that you are intelligent, motivated and imaginative, and that you can communicate ideas clearly in a range of formats. English graduates can write elegantly and persuasively, and can work either under their own steam or as part of a team. Perhaps most significantly, English graduates are able to think 'outside the box', using their research to find answers to challenging problems, and they have good time-management skills.

English graduates often go on to have careers in teaching and education; writing and publishing; PR and advertising; TV and media; journalism; acting; legal, financial and sales work; management or administration; or on to further study. Whatever subject or combination of subjects you have chosen to study at degree level, we hope this guide helps you navigate your way through one of the most challenging, yet hopefully inspirational, times of your life.

Devon Campbell-Hall

Part One
English Language

ENGLISH LANGUAGE: YEAR ONE
Terry McDonough

Introduction

This chapter will consider what language is, as well as discussing what people presume language to be. Subsequently, we will look at how language is studied and discuss some hints and tips for how you can be a successful English language student. There will also be helpful advice from previous students, whose comments greatly influenced the construction of this chapter.

> I wish I had known more about the language modules before I started the first year, especially the importance of historical context!
>
> (Zoe, Year One, BA English Language)

Quick! Come here! Listen to me for a moment. I'm going to tell you a few secrets about the wonderful world of language. I'm going to tell you about a lot of things we take for granted and don't always have time to communicate in our lectures. I'm going to give you a roadmap that will help you survive your first year as a language student and beyond. You see, I asked my students what they would have liked to have seen in an introductory guide, the advice that really helped them, as well as the things they learned the hard way. I'm not going to tell you what you already know or what you'll find in every other introductory guide. No. I'm going to tell you the things you might not hear elsewhere. Here's what we're going to do:

1. We're going to discuss what language actually is and how many of us make big assumptions about its nature.

2. We're going to have a look at what we call linguistics and how these linguistic types study this stuff we call language.

3. We're going to go through a few tips – advice that really works and will make a big difference to how successful you are.

If you're ready, we'll get started. There's no point wasting words or thanking my neighbour's cat. These are the tips you won't get elsewhere. Grab your backpack and your boots. We're heading into the jungle. You might want to pack a machete too.

Adapting to University Life

Starting anything new fills each of us with anxiety from the first day of high school, college or sixth form to beginning a new job or moving into a new home. Starting university is no different but, rest assured, it will be the first day of the most incredible experience of your life. Not only will you meet new, lifelong friends and enjoy a host of new, and exciting, experiences, you will also enter into the only phase in your life when you can take the time to indulge in the study of a subject that you are truly passionate about.

Studying language is an exciting and interesting opportunity. It is different from studying other subjects because language is all around us: it breathes within us and lives in the world outside of us. The more you learn about it, the more intrigued you become about its puzzles and intricacies, the more you will see its influence in your everyday life. This is, perhaps, the most important thing to remember – language is everywhere. It doesn't just live between the pages of a textbook. Language is life and you are about to become a part of that life.

Some practicalities. You might be worried about getting 'lost in the crowd' if you're at a large university. The best bet here is to join in with social groups – there might be a language society! Or even start your own study group (less exciting but practical). Get involved right from the beginning and you'll start to feel like you belong. Student populations at university are expanding and if you're homesick or have any other personal concerns, seek out the counselling service. There is one at every institution. Quite often there are helplines as well if you want to speak to someone anonymously. It's interesting to note that students coming from college often find that after six months that homesickness eases. They've learned how to microwave beans as well as having the freedom to eat cheese toasties at 2:00 a.m. Mature students – expect to feel guilty. Expect to try and be Wonder Woman or Superman. Expect to wish that Beatle's song was true and there was eight days in a week. You'll adapt and those you care for will adapt with you. It's difficult but doable – we see the stories and the mini-triumphs at every graduation ceremony. Yours will be one of them.

Remember also that if you need help with study skills there are often extra classes (sometimes optional, sometimes built into the course) you can take advantage of. If you have any additional requirements, for example you are dyslexic or feel you would benefit from being assessed, make an appointment with student services. It's important to get the ball rolling with this as early as possible. Some students might be partnered with scribes or note takers, or be given additional support to help brush up their English skills if they speak another language. Help is out there, you just need to ask. Finally, take advantage of your lecturers' office hours. They'll be posted on the door or on their staff pages – that's what they're there for. Last word of advice before we get cracking – be careful of those pounds. Any bursary you might get is for books (there will be many), not for the pub. Stagger it too – many of our students have become panicked after spending their bursaries in the first week or so. It's for the year! Ask student services in advance whether your institution has similar financial help for students. Get a penny jar.

What Is Language?

This is the first question I ask. There's usually silence. A tumbleweed rolls across the floor. Somewhere in the distance a lone coyote howls. The silence kills me. Not one brave hand. First-day nerves, I think. I haven't just fallen into a Sergio Leone western. I inevitably send around a plain envelope so they can offer their definitions on slips of paper. I feel like I'm collecting teeth. I think it's only polite that you do the same. No, I don't want you to collect teeth. I want you to tell me what language is. Go on, I'm listening.

Task – Complete the sentence: Language is …

Now, imagine you're folding the slip of paper and placing it in my envelope. We'll get to the 'answer' in a moment but we first need to have a think about what I've just done. Did you notice what I was doing?

I just sent you a message from the past. It's not a recording of what's happening to me right now but the subjective memory of a moment I experienced prior to writing this. I'm almost acting as a relay for a moment in my past in an attempt to express an idea to you, a person in some unknown future. For all I know this future moment – the moment when you read this chapter – could be years, even decades, from when I wrote it. I will never know if my idea has been communicated but I can at least be sure that I expressed it. I'm addressing you directly though, in the present tense. I'm making this happen *now*. I've either mastered space and time, or there's something both peculiar and amazing about this thing we call language. It's almost magical, and we might label much of that magic as metaphor. Some would say that metaphor characterizes how we think and communicate. I drew upon the domain of the spaghetti western with its tumbleweeds and howling coyotes to illustrate the barren wasteland which is that first lecture when everyone is still acclimatizing. I also mentioned collecting teeth. It would literally be quite sinister if it was true, but we accept that this is a metaphor that signifies a difficult task. (Or perhaps you imagined me as the tooth fairy?)

Overall, I have used language to my advantage, to colour a scenario and highlight an important question, but I have also been used by my language because I have been obliged, forced even, to codify the muddle in my mind into a series of intelligible sound-symbols. Our relationship with our language is one of intimacy with our world. If you had never heard of a spaghetti western, Sergio Leone or the folklore surrounding the tooth fairy, then my metaphors would have fallen flat and my language would have failed me. I would have failed to communicate my thoughts even though I used our common tongue.

For now, back to that first question: what is language? I have your answer in my envelope.

So you think you know what language is?

Every year, without exception, the most common definition from students is that language is a tool for communication, something so common and everyday that it's barely worth thinking about. Even dogs have it, apparently, or so one of my students believed. Whilst language might be one of the ways in which we communicate, in which we express our thoughts, our desires and our needs, it is by no means simply an interchangeable tool for communication. Sometimes, as we discussed in the previous paragraph, language can fail to communicate anything at all. Language seems to exist both inside of us – as the stuff of memory and conscious thought – and outside of us – as the header on a letter or the words on this page. Language is so powerful that it can convince us of things that aren't true and even get us into trouble. It seems to be everywhere and it seems to come from everywhere. If we could hover above the earth and see human activity as a whole we would see that much of that activity is linguistic, from the father in Kenya teaching his child a song, to the astronaut aboard the ISS remembering when she first learned to sing.

Language is never a nothing, or a something; it is our everything. It came before us. It will be here when we're gone. If you are not convinced, then think about what we have just done, you and I together. We've traversed space and time to create a meeting of minds. We will never meet. We will probably never even pass in the street yet here we are together, you and I, thinking and talking across space and time. It's amazing, don't you think? Language is the genome of our civilization. That's the answer. But that's what you placed in my envelope, isn't it?

Why does language make us special?

Chimpanzees frequently use tools. When necessary, an orang-utan can walk upright. The orca whale even has some semblance of culture. Not one of these sophisticated, advanced species has a language. Yes, they can communicate (I speak limited chimpaneese) but we have yet to demonstrate their possession of a language. We have yet to come across a dolphin telling a porpoise about the finer details of existential finology, or a bonobo chimp telling a gorilla how to construct a house from bamboo. A language, you see, is defined by the possession of a **grammar**: by a set of rules, an agreed series of organizing principles common to all language users. Despite the variety of human language systems, the possession of a **grammar** is universal and not too dissimilar, bound as it is by our embodied experience of a shared world. Whether our first language is Cantonese, Swahili or Gaelic, we experience the world in much the same way. We (the subject) all experience (the verb/predicate) the world (the object) in the same way (the adverbial). How we interpret, understand and describe this experience is another thing altogether.

Isn't this all common sense?

Our common attitude to language is one big assumption. We might even say that our informed attitudes to language are, to a certain degree, based on a series of assumptions. Everybody has an opinion about language. The correct or incorrect use of language is a political topic which still has a degree of currency. You only need to glance at the comments section below a news article to witness individuals correcting one another on their spelling or use of grammar. It can all seem so mundane and technical, so commonplace. Studying language is very different from this. The more you study it, the more it wriggles beneath your microscope, the more you will realize how elusive it is. Here's an example: we all know what the colour blue is, right? It's a common primary colour. You might be able to see it right now. We might define the colour 'blue' as the frequency of light visible at 610–70 THz on the optical spectrum. But how might we describe the quality of the colour blue? We can conjure up a simile – blue like the sky, like her dress, like the colour of your eyes – but we're only talking about the quality of the colour blue in terms of something else. We are only making a comparison which leads us to another challenge.

Task – Can you describe the quality of the colour blue without making reference to something else? Go on, give it a go.

Okay then, I'm guessing that no matter how hard you tried, however many ways you bent the premise, the description of the quality of the colour blue became a little tricky. I mean, how do we even know that we each see the same quality when we look at the colour defined as blue? Maybe the quality I perceive as red is the quality you perceive as blue. It's a circular question that can't be answered through linguistic investigation. It's a point where linguistic investigation (describe the quality of the signifier 'blue') unearths a philosophical question. This is not uncommon. Our preoccupation with language, with what it is and what it does, with where it came from and where it might go, has all arisen from the philosophical tradition. In fact, there is nothing more discussed or deliberated in the history of philosophy than the form and nature of language. It is one of the few spaces where philosophical enquiry meets scientific investigation. Here are a few more linguistic puzzles for you to ponder:

- Exactly how many needles of hay do we need to make a 'pile of hay'?

- Can you define what is 'good' without referring to what is 'bad'?

- Why isn't a 'toothbrush' called a 'teethbrush'?

- How might we define auxiliary verbs (be, can, could, do, have, may, might, must, shall, should, will, would) without using lexical verbs (run, jump, smile)?

Where did all these ideas come from?

As linguists, our ideas emerged, as they still do, from philosophy. However, our approach is congruent with the scientific method. By rights, contemporary linguistics emerged towards the end of the nineteenth century from the blending of **philology** with the concerns of **continental philosophy** and was later co-opted in the mid-twentieth century by what we refer to as **analytic philosophy**. There has been a bit of a disagreement between **continental philosophers** and **analytic philosophers** ever since and we now refer to ideas from continental philosophy as the **philosophy of language,** whilst ideas from analytic philosophy are often referred to as **linguistic philosophy**. Confusing? I agree. Avoid choosing sides, though, and aim to see the merits of each. Choosing sides often leads to fanaticism, which will only cloud your thinking. Many people passionately support a football team. By supporting a team you can only ever see the sport from that team's perspective. If you avoid supporting a team you can see the beauty of the sport for what it is, rather than from a perspective obscured by your own position.

If you want to delve into the philosophical context which underpins linguistics, then there are two texts which I would consider essential. The first is the renowned introductory text called *Philosophy Made Simple* (1981) by Richard Popkin and Avrum Stroll, and the second is *Philosophy for Linguists* (2000) by Siobhan Chapman. Whilst Chapman focuses exclusively on the analytic tradition, Popkin and Stroll provide a fairly balanced introduction to both the analytic and continental traditions.

What's This Linguistics, Then?

The hardest thing about the course was the sheer volume, and complexity, of theories about the evolution of language, from neuroscience to behaviourism. This was difficult to grasp in the first few months.

(Gideon, Year Three, BA English Language and History)

Linguistics is the scientific study of human language. Modern linguistics emerged from the posthumous publications of **Ferdinand de Saussure**, most notably his *Course in General Linguistics* (1916), a compendium of notes organized and published by his students. Saussure, whilst teaching philology, ended his lectures with his own ideas, and his biggest contribution was the notion that we should move away from studying how language changes over time (diachronic analysis) to how we perceive language as a phenomenon, and to what language actually does right now (synchronic analysis). Saussure's approach is referred to as **structural linguistics**, whilst some of his ideas are still studied in the field of **semiotics** (the study of signs). Saussure is also regarded as the founder of the school of thought known as **structuralism**, which has had a tremendous impact on academia as a whole. Not bad for a man who decided to discuss his ideas with his students after class!

Following the publication of Saussure's *Course in General Linguistics*, synchronic or structural linguistics came to be defined as a new science. We define it as scientific because language can be recorded, measured and analysed; ideas about language can be tested and those ideas can then be falsified. This is the main distinction in approach from, say, studying literature. We can't measure or falsify any particular interpretation of a literary text. We can, though, describe a literary text in terms of its composition and our descriptive results probably won't be too dissimilar, even though our ideas about interpretation might be radically different. As linguists, we aim to describe what *is* evident rather than ascribe a value to what *might* be evident. However, discussing literary narratives is one fairly small branch of the family. You see, linguistics is more of an umbrella term for a wide range of individual approaches and disciplines which each take language as a central concern. We can divide these approaches into three broad fields: **theoretical linguistics**, **applied linguistics** and **descriptive linguistics**.

Theoretical linguistics

This is the engine of language study. Theoretical linguistics is concerned with the study of universal categories, of the properties which all human languages share. All human languages have a grammar (an agreed series of rules), they all have a sound system, and they all, in some way, make meaning. As linguists we can examine these building blocks accordingly, which allows us to work towards building up our knowledge of linguistic universals. The cornerstone to this understanding is the study of **grammar**. When we study grammar we study the rules that govern the production of language composition. We might look at **syntax**, the structure of a sentence, its clauses and phrases. We might look at **morphology**, the internal structure and function of individual words. Or we might choose to look at **phonology**, the sound system of the language. When we begin to think about how meaning is made, how these structures make sense to anyone, we begin to think about **semantics**, the study of meaning. We might also situate these structures within particular contexts by taking into account the **pragmatic** function of language. It all makes sense when you think about it: if we are to understand the phenomenon of language, we need to first understand its mechanics. We need a way to describe its individual structures, from sound to word to phrase to clause to sentence, and we need to develop ways of understanding how these elements work together to communicate meaning (as well as the ways in which they might obscure meaning) in a particular context.

Okay. We need to return to the topic of **grammar** for a moment. Resist the temptation to throw this book into the fire and run screaming for the hills. Due to grammar's pivotal role in structuring human language, it has become a central concern in the field of linguistics and, like most big concerns in academia, there are a few different opinions on how we should approach it. Most of these opinions are formed on the bedrock of two grammatical frameworks and you are likely to encounter each of these in some form or another. The first is referred to as **transformational** or **generative grammar** (sometimes even **transformational-generative grammar**) which emerged from the work of **Noam Chomsky**. The second is referred to as **systemic functional grammar** and is based on the work of **Michael Halliday**. Both Chomsky and Halliday are considered forces of nature in the field of linguistics and it is good advice to pay considerable attention to their ideas. There are, of course, a few other grammatical frameworks, but none have had the same degree of impact. Whilst the texts themselves can be incredibly difficult for beginners, it is worthwhile familiarizing yourself with the similarities and differences within these models. Try using a secondary reader to help summarize these models. Understanding grammar and the dominant grammatical frameworks is essential to the understanding of **theoretical linguistics.**

Applied linguistics

This branch of linguistics, in contrast to theoretical linguistics, is concerned with real-world problems and the investigation of solutions to those problems. It arose in part as a response to the Chomskyan revolution in the 1960s, as an antidote to the highly abstract focus of **generative grammar.** Whilst this has a place in applied linguistics you might find that the work of Halliday asserts more of an influence. Applied linguistics is, as Halliday said, concerned with what language does rather than what language is. You will encounter disciplines such as discourse analysis (the social function of speech and interaction in context), language acquisition and emergent literacy (how infants and children acquire and develop language skills), second language acquisition (how bi- and multilingual speakers function in society) and stylistics (the linguistic analysis of literary texts). Regardless of your programme of study you will most likely find that **applied linguistics** plays a large role. It is also worth noting that when we set the *approach* aside we will often find that **applied linguistics** draws many of its techniques from **theoretical linguistics**, especially in terms of the analytical work. For instance, when we perform a stylistic analysis of a fictional text we look at each level of language (syntax, phonology, semantics, etc.) in much the same way as in **theoretical linguistics.** The difference, given away by the name, is that applied linguists look at language in application, rather than in isolation.

Descriptive linguistics

This brand of linguistics is the one you are already familiar with. It most likely formed the basis of your previous studies in linguistics. **Descriptive linguistics** is concerned with how language is used by speech communities in much the same way as **applied linguistics.** The difference is that descriptive linguistics is not concerned with real-world problems but is content with objective description. Its aim is to provide an adequate description of language. Etymology, the history of words and meaning, is considered a branch of descriptive linguistics.

Altogether now

We've only sketched the outlines of these three major approaches in the text above, but it is worth noting that you will rarely encounter such a distinction on an undergraduate programme. You will encounter each of the 'big three' in conjunction, and often under different names, or masked by different approaches. For example, I teach systemic functional grammar through the lens of stylistics. I tell my students much later on that they have actually been studying grammar, as the very mention of the term grammar seems to spread terror. However, it is always worth noting the distinction between these disciplines and this will become apparent as your studies continue.

What do linguists actually do?

Our primary job as linguists is to describe. Language is already here. We needn't synthesize it in a test tube, or deduce its probability from an equation, because it is within us and it is all around us. We need to record it, describe it and then, the tricky part, interpret the results. It's quite similar to how you might have dissected and labelled the parts of a plant in high school biology. We don't memorize dictionaries, guard our national heritage or decide how people should or shouldn't use language. These kinds of political attitudes are known as prescriptive and have no place in contemporary linguistics. As a newly minted linguist you are now prohibited from correcting people on the Internet. It's much more interesting to let everyone use language as they choose. This lets our language grow and change to suit many different needs. It also allows our language to begin to change us. Trying to dictate what language should be is like trying to dictate the shape of water. It isn't going to happen any time soon, so leave the prescriptivists to build bridges out of water. Our job is to sit on the embankment and watch them fall down.

Who does it?

We call prominent (or infamous) figures in the world of popular culture celebrities. These individuals are the most exposed or marketed and have often contributed to that area of life in some significant degree. They might have pioneered a new style of music, delivered an awe-inspiring performance or managed to film that unfilmable novel. And yes, I hear you – they might have done nothing much at all! Academia, for better or worse, is no different. There's a small group of A-listers, the real heavyweights; a steady pantheon of B-listers, often developing the work of the A-list; and then there's the rest of us, the nearly-theres and wannabes. It can be useful to make this distinction because, as you learn and develop, you will begin to see the people and their work in much the same way as you might see your favourite band and their discography.

We've already alluded to three of the key contributors to the field in Ferdinand de Saussure, Noam Chomsky, and M. A. K. Halliday. We might also pay attention to Fillmore, Croft, Leech and Crystal. Here are a few other big players in the disciplines that you are most likely to encounter on an undergraduate programme. I could have given you a reading list like any other book, but I think it's important that you find the work of your own accord.

Child language acquisition: Lev Vygotsky, B. F. Skinner, Paulo Freire, Jean Piaget, Noam Chomsky, Jerome Bruner.

Cognitive linguistics: George Lakoff, Mark Johnson, Thomas Givon, William Croft, David Cruise, Gilles Fauconnier, Mark Turner.

Communication: Roman Jakobson, Claude Shannon, Basil Bernstein, Charles Peirce, Daniel Chandler.

Critical discourse analysis: Norman Fairclough, Roger Fowler, Paul Chilton, Ruth Wodak, Teun van Dijk, Teun van Leeuwen.

Philosophy of language: John Locke, George Berkeley, David Hume, Martin Heidegger, Hans-Georg Gadamer, Ludwig Wittgenstein, John Searle, J. L. Austin, Jacques Derrida, Daniel Dennett.

Sociolinguistics: William Labov, Basil Bernstein, Robin Lakoff, Deborah Tannen, Deborah Cameron, Janet Holmes, Peter Trudgill.

Stylistics: Roman Jakobson, Geoffrey Leech, Mick Short, Roger Fowler, David Crystal, Elena Semino, Leslie Jeffries, Katie Wales, Paul Simpson.

Check out some of these people and familiarize yourself with their work. I can guarantee that you will come across many, if not all, of them. I can also guarantee that your lecturers' own work will be based on the work of those listed above. They are names that are going to become as familiar to you as any celebrity persona.

Why do we bother?

This is, sadly, another all-too-common question. What's the point? Why bother? Must we list *all* the transitive verbs in a Beckett monologue? We might be a little dismissive and say that studying the effect of point of view in a play doesn't really contribute new knowledge to the world or offer us anything of value. This view would undermine the important work that linguists do.

- Linguists work on the development of artificial intelligence systems and computer algorithms which form the bedrock of the technological systems which govern our daily lives, from how Google works to air traffic control and the latest missile defence systems.

- Linguists study cognitive impairments and brain damage in the hope of assisting those who suffer from such deficits. They also do extensive work with children in terms of how they learn and how they might overcome any developmental deficits. Linguists have a tremendous impact on education systems around the globe.

- Linguists operate as forensic scientists and their evidence is permissible in a court of law. We can identify the authors of death threats and ransom notes, detect culpability in criminal activity, and reconstruct conversations from diverse data sets. Linguists also play a role as analysts for intelligence services and they help protect us from those 'known unknowns'.

Linguists play a major role in the modern world and it is important to understand that this work has its basis in the science of linguistic description. We ask you to detail all the transitive verbs in a Beckett play because you might one day be programming the latest AI to use them, or giving precise evidence in a court of law.

How Do I Survive?

> The amount of reading and the workload in general that I was presented with was definitely overwhelming at first. The degree takes up the majority of my time, whether it's general reading, assignments, seminar tasks or revising for exams, but I must say it is all worth it!
>
> (Siddiqa, Year Two, BA English Language)

There's an entire industry built around the publication of study skills and learning methods. Many of these texts are invaluable and most will remind you of the importance of time management, note taking and the effective use of resources (including how to accurately reference those resources). We will avoid those topics as best we can since they are covered in much more detail elsewhere and in future chapters. Instead, here we will discuss a range of tips drawn from actual student experiences, things that have really worked for language students in the past. Most of these tips are drawn from actual discussions in tutorial groups and seminar workshops.

Learning tips

Relate what you are learning to your own experiences. You already do this every day. There is probably something you have a real passionate interest in and I bet you effortlessly know everything about that subject and can discuss it at length without much effort. We all have that friend who knows every detail about their favourite sports team, can recite every victory over the past 20 years, but may know little else. This is because the subject has real-world currency and is highly relevant due to a learned interest. The subject you are studying needs to be just as relevant. If you attend lectures thinking only of the end goal – the degree, the graduation, the after party – then you will find it difficult to make anything stick. You need to relate what you learn to your daily life. With language this is remarkably easy because it's already everywhere.

Make connections between the subject areas. This is especially important if you are studying a combination of subjects. Language is an incredibly promiscuous subject, quite happy to spend the night with anyone of interest. Think about how it fits with the companion discipline you have chosen. Let your technical understanding of grammar inform your creative writing. Use linguistic analyses to support your literary interpretations. Try transcribing conversational data to add depth to your sociological investigation, or to illustrate a point in political theory. Language has a role in all disciplines that have a relation to the human condition.

Always evaluate and criticize new ideas. It doesn't matter if you're listening to a peer or reading the latest paper from an emeritus professor of the known universe, you are simply listening to, or reading, the perspectives of another person. Don't fall into the trap of personality or authority by believing that any idea or position is immutable. Think for yourself: read, listen and evaluate from a critical perspective. Play devil's advocate. Read *against* a text. Look for questions rather than confirmations. A quick search on Google will show you that there are compelling arguments for the existence of interdimensional lizard-like aliens, cities thriving at the earth's core or a vast conspiracy of ancient vampires intent on ruling the world. I made that last one up, but you get the point. No matter how compelling the argument, there is no necessity for truth. What is truth anyway? We demonstrated earlier that we can't even be sure about the quality of the colour 'blue'. How can we be so sure about anything else? Live by Descartes' mantra – accept that you exist as a thinking being and treat all else as speculation, no matter the source.

Think and daydream at every opportunity. Imagination is a powerful tool and our mind's capacity for invention is endless. Albert Einstein chanced upon the idea behind his special theory of relativity whilst daydreaming about how it would feel to surf a wave of light. Creative examples permeate Einstein's work from the description he used involving a moving train to explain general relativity (the primary object is always relative to a secondary coordinate) to his discussion of identical twins travelling through space to explain special relativity (the twin travelling at light speed around the sun would experience less time – therefore age less – than the twin on Earth). Take Einstein's example as a lead and let your imagination roam around the ideas you encounter. How would it feel to surf a sentence on a word?

Tell others what you have learned. My harder-working friends often remind me that I get paid for talking about things that interest me. This is essentially what teaching is. When we teach, we tell another what we ourselves have learned. It is the best way to learn because it forces us to think about what we know, and the order of what we know. Tell somebody else what you have learned.

Pace yourself throughout the year. Each semester is like an 800-metre relay. The intensity of the workload will ebb and flow, starting fairly gradually before building to a crescendo towards the end of each semester, when you will have multiple assignments to submit as well as seminar tasks to complete alongside all your other commitments in life. You need to become a relay runner. Start each semester at a steady pace, plan and prepare for the topic at hand, before building to a sprint towards the end. Strangely, and from experience, most students do the opposite. They start the semester like lightning but usually end up frazzled towards the end. Always pace yourself.

Play the game. This is the tip I shouldn't include. As an undergraduate, pondering the philosophy section of the onsite Waterstones, my then year tutor sidled up beside me and told me this: 'Put those philosophy books down,' she said, 'and learn to play the game.' It was a piece of advice that stuck with me and it played a big part in my success as an undergraduate. It's easy to get sidetracked, caught up in little details or lost in distant avenues when you study a subject like language. You must remain focused on your objective. Continually remind yourself that you are following a formal programme of study. It isn't enlightenment, it isn't an intellectual voyage, it isn't anything other than what it says in the course documentation. Learning and achieving should always be your primary objectives, but such virtuous aims have no weight without a strategy. You might well have discovered something truly groundbreaking but your efforts will only be rewarded if they meet the aims of the course. Familiarize yourself with those aims and make sure that your learning strategy meets them. Doing otherwise is like trying to cook without a recipe. You might have flavour, ideas that would make your dish the most delicious in the world, but if you can't use the oven then it might all go horribly wrong.

Reading

Check the contents and index first for relevant information. There is really no need to read a textbook from cover to cover unless it is a particularly seminal piece of work. Use each textbook as a resource. Be selfish – take what you need and leave the rest on the shelf. By checking the contents page and the index you can familiarize yourself with the contents of a book and source the information that you require – for example, whatever chapter or paragraph is relevant to your work.

Make journal articles and research papers a priority. This is how the academic world operates. Papers are presented at conferences for peer review before submission to one of the many academic journals within each discipline. Whilst textbooks are a fantastic source of secondary information, often serving as an introduction or a composite of different sources, journals and articles offer more specificity and depth. Journals are also more current and they are generally published each quarter. A textbook on the other hand, however new, may have taken two to three years before it reaches publication. Give current information priority. Take advantage of any session that the university library holds regarding access and research. Journals should become your closest friends as you develop as an academic.

Reading complex texts is a skill. The more you read, the easier it becomes. You may feel as though you have landed on an alien planet the first time you encounter theoretical writing. Don't be too alarmed. Once you are familiar with the language of a text – its vernacular, if you will – the reading experience will become easier. It's easy to feel overwhelmed by complex texts, especially translations, but remember these are only words written by another person. If a text is difficult it is often down to poor, obscure writing rather than a total lack of understanding on your part. Some academics (yes, you, Lacan) might choose to write in a dense, obtuse style in order to project an image of intellectual superiority. Don't doubt yourself straight away. Sometimes you should doubt the validity of the author.

Read widely: 'English' is a multidisciplinary subject. In fact, 'English' is the name attributed to the study of language and literature in the Anglo-American world. Whilst English studies is a legitimate subject area, what you will encounter as 'English' is linguistics and literary studies. We have already discussed the range of subjects which overlap with contemporary linguistics, so take advantage of this opportunity. It is an opportunity to learn diversity and encounter a myriad of interesting ideas. Dip into sociology, psychology, cognitive science, evolutionary biology, neuroscience, philosophy – they all help us with the puzzle of language, consciousness and the mind and play a part in understanding what it means to be human.

Read. Read. Read. Keep reading and then read some more. Read like a sugar addict in Willy Wonka's chocolate factory. Devour everything. Knowledge doesn't come with calories.

Writing

Writers write. Writing assignments and getting your thoughts across in a clear and structured way can be challenging at first. The more you write, the better you'll get. This is the golden rule. Writing is a skill, a higher-order cognitive skill, but nevertheless a skill. At some point in our childhood each of us learned to ride a bike. We didn't consult a textbook or attend a course, no matter how many times those knees and elbows scraped the floor. We practised and practised until we got it right, or at least until we stopped hitting the concrete. Imagine if we had pondered the process of bike riding, amassed all the tips in the world – would we have learned to ride the bike? Not likely. We learned to ride through riding, just as we learn to write through writing. The more we do it, the less bloody we are likely to get.

In order to get better at writing, you first need a space to write – not a physical space but an area that acts as a canvas for your thoughts. You could keep a journal to record your daily reflections, start a blog to discuss the things you've read or maybe start writing that e-book on underwater basket weaving. The content isn't as important as the process. If you're writing, you're getting better at writing and this will improve the quality of your assignments. Would a musician improve if they only played their instrument half a dozen times a year? No. Never. They would only improve if they played every day, whether busking in the street or covering a classic track for a friend. The pen, pencil or keyboard is your instrument and the words are your musical notes, notes containing infinite possibilities. It's kind of beautiful when you think of it like that.

Consider the assignment question *carefully.* We composed the question *very carefully* with a series of specific learning outcomes in mind. In late summer each year I spend several hours preparing my assignment briefs (lists of questions) and texts for my students whilst considering the module's outcomes alongside my own expectations. I make sure that the questions emerge from the content in my lectures and that the content in my lectures informs the expectations of the assessed questions. I expect my students to demonstrate their understanding of the topics covered in the lecture theatre, but I also leave enough room for their own thoughts and ideas and the questions allow for this. There's nothing better than actually learning something new from student papers and it is often these students – those who demonstrate their understanding of the basics in conjunction with their own perspective – who achieve success. Students who fail to answer the question, or who simply recite lecture notes collected in class, will sadly achieve a lesser degree of success.

Visualize information and ideas. We are visual creatures and we live in a highly visual culture. From the variety of media forms to our preoccupation with physical appearance, how something looks carries a high degree of meaning. By visualizing the material you encounter and learn you are converting it into a different mode, belonging to a different realm of the senses. You are processing information and consolidating memory. Those little dendrites in your brain are getting stronger. Try using mind maps, lists or posters. It is possible to reduce an entire text to a simple A4 sheet of visuals. A picture paints a thousand words; several pictures can encompass an entire book!

Create a plan, like a roadmap that will guide you as you write. Spontaneous lyricism is wonderful in creative prose but academic writing demands logic and precision. You need a plan, a little pathway designed to guide your prospective reader through the terrain of your ideas. I started my contribution to this book in much the same way. I thought about the objective (essential information for first-year language students), I undertook the research (others' opinions, my own teaching practice, my students' experiences) then I opened a document on my laptop and worked out the road map – what places we must visit, how we would reach them, and in what order. The result was a series of subheadings: a series of signposts for the reader and prompts for my future writing-self. As a bonus, it breaks the writing down into smaller tasks, which can be a huge psychological boon if you are faced with composing a large text. An assignment is never a 2,500-word lump of text; it is a series of 500-word steps. It's a sightseeing tour rather than a breathless marathon.

It's all in the editing. That poor, lonely, first draft is a prototype. It is closed to the world. Nobody but you will ever read it. If you have made a few headings to guide your thoughts (and the reader) as suggested above, the next step is to fill in each section with the notes you have accumulated through research. Write as you will, get it all down on the page, and worry about form later. Once you have a loose structure and some insight into your ideas you can use the editing process as an opportunity to craft your writing. One of the best things you can do is read the first draft aloud. It will allow you to see any inconsistencies, clunky sentences and unsupported claims. Language is primarily an artefact of speech and sound. Staring at words on a page moves away from your natural ability to use and produce language. By reading aloud, you focus on the spoken word and the spoken word is something that our brains can naturally tune into. Think how often you recognize inconsistencies or errors in speech without even trying.

Read your way out of 'writer's block'. I often hear about the terror of staring at a blank document wondering where that amazing essay is going to emerge from. We all use the term 'writer's block' as though something nasty is trapped in the ol' neuro-pipes. There is no such thing as writer's block though.

It is simply fear masquerading as something else. The fear of failure, the fear of precision, the fear that what you are doing will be a disappointment. Put all that to one side and just write your assignments. Write what and how you like. You will edit later. As we've discussed, nobody else will see this early process. However, if acknowledging your fear – calling it out for what it is – doesn't quite work for you then try reading your favourite academic, someone who really appeals to you. This will often get your brain into academic writing mode, and whilst the first few paragraphs may be wholly derivative of what you have just read, you will soon fall into your own rhythm. We each have our own style, pace and rhythm. Find yours and use it. Be assured that it will gradually emerge: simply focus on the truth and allow your natural talent to emerge. You are the only one in the world who can write like that. If you've followed the tips above – read the question, designed a road-map – then it should be a breeze, a case of simply filling in the gaps by working in your sources and arguments. Good luck!

2

ENGLISH LANGUAGE: YEAR TWO
Val Jessop

Introduction

Welcome to Year Two. In this chapter, I will consider the difference between the expectations your tutors have of you at this level and those of the previous year. You will understand what learning outcomes are, as well as terms like 'exit velocity'. In addition, you will gain advice on bibliographies and referencing. There will be examples from students that demonstrate successful answers to exam questions, as well as those that need more work. You will undertake simple but effective tasks that will help increase your own awareness of what is required of you at this stage of your academic career, such as how to 'signpost' an essay.

Achieving at Level 5

So far, your assignments in Year One should have provided you with the basic skills to study language and should have given you all the analytical 'tools' you need to perform more complex tasks that will be asked of you in Year Two. Your tutors will be assessing you at a different level now, and this can be scary, as from this point on your marks will begin to determine your final award. First, there are some questions that you should be sure you know the answer to, for example:

How will my final award be calculated?

While the end of your degree may seem a long way off, you need to know whether or not your marks in Year Two are given the same amount of credit as those you will achieve in Year Three. Some programmes are equally weighted between the final two years, whereas other programmes may give more credit for marks achieved in Year Three to account for 'exit velocity'.

What is exit velocity?

This simply means that you will be improving academically as you progress through your programme of study, developing your writing style and your ability to handle complex ideas. As you get better at these things, your marks should gradually start to get higher so that by your final year you will be achieving at a higher level than in your first or second year. Some institutions recognize this and give you more credits for third year work than for second year work. If you are unsure, check with your course handbook or your personal tutor. We will return to this when we look at Year Three expectations in the next chapter.

Understanding the Levels: Year 2 / Level 5

So what are these 'levels' that you are expected to achieve and where do they come from? All educational institutions within the UK have to maintain a certain academic standard. This standard is set by the Quality Assurance Agency for Higher Education (QAA), which provides guidelines to which institutions refer, ensuring that all students achieve comparable standards of achievement before being given their award. You receive your qualification when you have achieved certain educational outcomes set by your tutors in accordance with the standards set down by the QAA. Naturally, as you progress through your studies these become a little more sophisticated, and the terms used to describe the 'learning outcomes' at each level reflect these increasing levels of achievement.

It's important then to understand what your tutor is looking for when he or she assesses your work. You are in Year Two now, also known as Level 5. As we progress academically we are assessed depending on the level we are expected to have attained at any point. You have already achieved Level 4 by passing your first year on the programme. Students who have achieved Level 4 are expected to be able to construct an argument based on their ability to weigh up possible methods of analysis, to identify an appropriate argument, and/or apply a theoretical model. Now that you have those skills, you need to be able to show that you can bring together competing arguments for talking about the same thing and assess which argument you find the most convincing and why. So your tutors this year will be assessing your ability to analyse, synthesize and evaluate. You will probably find some version of these words in your assessment briefs.

Learning Outcomes

For each of your assignments you will be probably be given not just the task, but a number of 'learning outcomes' which you have to achieve in order to gain a good mark. It's worth checking these carefully to ensure that you have done everything that's expected of you. It will also help you to remain focused. The learning outcomes will include a number of keywords which you should look out for, as these relate to skills that you need to be able to demonstrate at this level. You may find it helpful to underline these. Examples include:

- apply

- analyse

- evaluate

- produce

- demonstrate

- critique

- devise

Whereas last year you were demonstrating your understanding of the terms you were using and applying them, you will now start to explore alternative explanations, competing viewpoints, and a – sometimes confusing – amount of terminology and labels for concepts that seem to mean very similar things. This is because scholars are continually exploring and developing ideas suggested by other scholars and thinking about how useful they are, and whether they can be improved upon or adapted to another context. Sometimes academics even argue with one another! (If you want to see an example of a rather heated scholarly debate, see Stanley Fish, *Is There a Text in This Class?* (1982) and its subsequent criticisms). So what sort of tasks will you be expected to do now? Tutors work to a set of 'learning outcomes' for the modules they teach. They will be assessing whether the work you have submitted has achieved each of those outcomes, but you can check this yourself before you hand over your assignment.

Below is a list of learning outcomes from one of my Level 5 modules. I have underlined the key aspects that I assess when I mark students' work for this module.

Examples of learning outcomes from a Level 5 language module

Learning outcomes: Issues in Stylistics

By the end of this module you will be able to:

- **apply** and **discuss analytical** and **theoretical frameworks** in relation to a wide range of literary and non-literary texts;

- **evaluate** the usefulness of various analytical approaches for the discussion of literary and non-literary texts;

- **demonstrate** an awareness of the **link between text and context** of production and reception;

- produce written work which demonstrates communicative competence in oral and written skills, including the ability to **devise and sustain coherent argument**;

- **produce detailed and systematic** stylistic analyses of texts belonging to the three genres using **appropriate analytical frameworks**.

In other words, the student needs to be able to choose and apply an appropriate theoretical framework, and use it to analyse a text; discuss and evaluate its usefulness; consider the context of when and why the text was written and how that influences the language used and whether this has changed, and produce an essay that is well structured and coherent. If you can break down the elements that will be assessed in your work, as I have done here, you are well on your way to achieving a successful outcome.

Staying Focused

Once you have identified what you are expected to do in order to achieve the learning outcomes, make sure that you have answered the question set by the tutor and have answered all elements of the question. Students sometimes digress too far from the topic they are supposed to be answering, perhaps because they have become interested in something that isn't entirely relevant, or they have missed part of the question and therefore can't gain optimum marks. Keep reminding yourself of the question to ensure you remain on track. This applies also to any examination that you take. As mentioned in other sections, tutors might also start their question with a quotation. If this is the case, think about why they have chosen to do this. Usually, the quotation relates to a key element of the topic they want you to discuss, so always refer to this as well as the question itself.

In addition, you may be given some guidance on the marking criteria which your tutor will use when assessing your work. If you are not given these it's worth asking for them. That way you will be able to judge whether you have achieved to the best of your ability.

Exams

Make sure you know in advance what percentage of your marks will be assessed by exam and how much by coursework: what learning outcomes are being assessed by exams and which by coursework, and make sure you have answered all parts of the question. Too many students fail to achieve better marks despite being thoroughly prepared for exams because they have anticipated the question they think will be asked in the exam, and answer *that* question rather than the one that's actually on the paper.

Rather than anticipating and preparing answers, revise for exams as if you are preparing for an essay. Conduct thorough background reading and don't just revise from lecture notes. Tutors can recognize their own words when they reappear in exam answers. If you've read widely it will help you to respond to *any* question in the area and this is much better than a prepared response. Try to acknowledge your sources, although remember you aren't expected to include page numbers, only accurate dates. Similarly if you're using a quotation from a secondary source, it's unlikely you'll be penalized if you haven't used the exact words, and quoting from secondary sources demonstrates your wider reading (but see the advice about word count and secondary sources below). Make sure you learn the correct spellings of key terms and theorists; incorrect spellings could suggest you don't know the area well enough or can't be bothered to learn them.

Revising with Your Friends

Discuss topics with your peers and form study groups by all means as this will help you to remember ideas. However, it's better to discuss the subject widely rather than to 'test' one another or only discuss lecture notes. One of the things that tutors are looking for is originality, and if you and your friends have all answered the same topics and come up with the same ideas and examples, then you won't score highly in that category. A better idea might be to each consider different areas to focus on and discuss a number of different topics from key texts recommended by your tutor. This has the advantage of helping you to prepare more thoroughly and in more depth.

You could try word association techniques: for example, you might take a topic such as point of view and write down everything that you know on that topic. Some of my students explored potential dissertation topic ideas by drawing a spider diagram outlining their initial ideas. They passed this on to friends to add their own thoughts.

This technique has the advantage of enabling you to share ideas, while allowing you to formulate your own opinion. Activities like these can help you to remember key points when you come to write your exam answers, but remember to include additional activities such as reading around topics discussed in class.

How to Be Original

You will have been given key texts, articles and readings by your tutor and you should ensure you read all of these. Your tutor will be looking for your ability to broaden your knowledge by adding to the information given in class. Try looking at the bibliographies of texts to see where their ideas have come from, or look at other disciplines to see if similar ideas have been explored from a different perspective. For example, ideas about language acquisition and development is an area that is covered by social psychology: influences on language change might be covered in history; discussion about viewpoint and perspective in literary texts might be worth exploring in literature about art. Ask your librarian for ideas and further help. We will look at originality in more detail when we discuss Year Three.

Don't Ignore the Basics

Bibliographies and referencing

Many students find referencing tedious and leave it to the last minute. Let's face it, it's not the most exciting thing you'll write during your course! However, you will be assessed on your ability to use academic conventions correctly, and inaccurate referencing can lead to an accusation of accidental plagiarism, which can be a serious offense. Referencing isn't the most difficult skill you'll learn and with a bit of practice you can soon master the technique of writing impressive bibliographies and supporting your writing with academic sources that are accurately referenced. Imagine if you had written a book or even a chapter in a book. You would want your contribution to be acknowledged and would be rather annoyed if you discovered that your ideas were felt to be interesting enough to be used by someone else, but the source of those ideas went unacknowledged. Referencing is easy once you have learned how to do it, and your institution will probably have a guide that you can follow to help you. It's important to master this skill early on as the further you progress through your academic career, the more expectations there will be that you will know how to do it correctly. Remember that by submitting assignments you are entering a discourse community, and need to show clearly how your work relates to key figures discussing and sharing ideas on that topic. Many students also worry about how to cite electronic sources. If those sources have a named author and date then you should cite them as you would a book before citing the web address and the date you accessed the information. Again, consult guidelines given to you by tutors.

The same goes for bibliographies. These should be on a separate sheet at the end of your essay with the works cited in alphabetical order, and this is easy enough to do. It's also easy to cause a tutor some impatience if your bibliography is tacked on at the end of the last page.

Referencing is easy once you have learned how to do it, and your institution will probably have a guide that can help you. It's important to master this skill early on as by Level 5 and 6 you will be expected to get it right and may be penalized if you don't.

Proofreading: Checking for sense and meaning

One of the more fun activities I do with my students is to provide them with sentences where the writer's unintentional ambiguity creates humour where none is intended. Here are some examples of newspaper headlines that I ask students to rewrite in order to clarify the writer's meaning:

PANDA MATING FAILS; VETERINARIAN TAKES OVER

STOLEN PAINTING FOUND BY TREE

DRUNK GETS NINE MONTHS IN VIOLIN CASE

(ALTA 2014)

Unfortunately, students sometimes don't recognize the ambiguity in their own sentences and don't realize that their meaning is unclear. It's worth checking for clarity in your work, and if you're not sure, ask someone else to read it through for you. It shouldn't matter if that person doesn't know anything about your topic. If you strive for clarity of expression, then your writing should be accessible to most people (see section on using theoretical frameworks for more on this). Sometimes we are so familiar with what we've written we don't notice any potentially ambiguous sentences.

Students' work sometimes lacks clarity due to using the wrong words for the context.

Example 1

Saussure originally created the theory to be completely mental.

The ambiguity arises here due to the use of the word 'mental', which in colloquial terms means 'mad' or 'crazy'. Presumably, this isn't the meaning intended by the student, and he or she intends to convey the fact that the theory refers to a mental or cognitive process. Perhaps a more successful rewording would be something like:

Saussure's ideas refer to processes which occur when a word evokes a mental concept.

Example 2

Two of the most popular eating disorders are anorexia and bulimia.

As with the first example, the problem here arises from the use of the adjective 'popular', which implies that people make a deliberate choice of eating disorders, when presumably the writer means 'common'.

Task – Identify the ambiguity in the following examples from student work. Can you help to clarify the meaning?

1. Forensic officers have analysed that the weapon used was a hand gun and that the body had not been sexually insulted.

2. The narrator describes how to the left and right men are being slaughtered in droves and as the narrative unfolds the reader is waiting for their turn to die.

3. As the English language evolved it would have to become standardized and have a clear structure before it was inflicted upon the rest of the world.

Spelling

Sometimes it isn't just key terms or unusual names that students have problems spelling. If you know you have a problem with spelling, check with a dictionary: don't rely on the spellchecker on your computer as it can't identify words that are not in common use, and it may substitute a different word or an Americanism. It also can't distinguish between homophones – words that sound the same but have different meanings such as pray/prey, hear/here or principle/principal. The latter example occurs surprisingly frequently in my students' writing, as in: 'The Cooperative Principal'. This example brings to mind the most important but obliging member of a college (a 'principal'), whereas the student is referring to Grice's (1975) cooperative principle of conversation, which is a proposition or theory of how conversation works in practice. Here are some more homophones. Try to work out the word the student intended to use: the correct spellings are included in parentheses. Make sure you proofread your exam answers carefully!

Barewolf was the first English epic poem [Beowulf].

Miss Havisham was jolted at the alter [jilted, altar].

The eyes are the mirror of the sole [soul].

Tautology

Tautology refers to statements such as 'War is war' or 'Boys will be boys' which appear to convey meaning even though they are ostensibly stating the obvious. Sometimes students create tautological sentences unintentionally and it is often difficult to work out exactly what it is they are trying to express.

Here is an example from a student's work:

The poem uses parallelism in its structure to create a parallel structure.

Here the writer is struggling to define parallelism and resorts to tautology as a result. If you are struggling to express something in your own words it suggests that you don't understand a concept enough to explain it. Go back to textbooks or your lecture notes and read around for deeper understanding so that you can express your ideas more clearly. If you are still unsure, ask your tutor to clarify the terms. You will probably find you aren't the only one who is a bit confused!

Task – Consider the following examples. Can you work out what the writer is trying to say? How would you express this more clearly?

1. The poet laureate includes poets who have entered the laureate.

2. English is widely spoken in Great Britain.

3. Numbers have been used. Examples include two, nine, three.

Comment

In 1), the sentence suggests that the writer doesn't really know what it means to be the poet laureate, so they should have looked up a definition first to enable them to be more clear and accurate. 'Laureate' refers to a person who has been recognized for their achievement. Demonstrating your understanding of the key terms being used in a discipline is crucial, so it's a good idea to keep a notebook or glossary with the terms and their meanings and keep refreshing your memory in advance of any exam. In 2), the student is probably struggling to write an introduction. The sentence sounds odd because it suggests that English is not the first language of Great Britain when of course it is. In 3), the student possibly wants to highlight a predominance of numbers in the text which have created an effect, but at the moment, it's unclear what this statement is adding to their argument! If you had difficulty trying to do the activity above I'm not surprised!

Examples such as 2) and 3) often occur when a student begins writing without a plan for their answer or is struggling to begin writing. The person marking the paper is likely to skip over sentences such as these as they convey little meaning so are a waste of already limited time. It's worth planning carefully the points you want to make before you begin writing in exams to make the most of the time allowed.

Using Theoretical Frameworks

Studying language requires students to refer to the work of a number of critics who have created models or frameworks for explaining linguistic features. In Year One (Level Four) you will have been introduced to a number of these, and this knowledge set will be expanded upon as you progress to Levels Five and Six. In addition, you will now be expected to consider the usefulness of the work of different academics and any shortcomings in that work. This requires the ability to assess the merits of that work, not just criticizing any weaknesses or omissions. At this level, you will be expected to apply linguistic frameworks/theories or models to texts in order to do this.

However, a common error made by students is to write as if the authors of novels or plays have knowledge of the same frameworks, and exploit these to create effects. Remember, such frameworks have been developed to help us to interpret effects in accordance with what we know about language and we apply them to texts – they aren't inherently there.

Explain before Applying

It's important to explain the theories you are using before applying them to your text. You may feel that this isn't necessary – after all, your tutor already knows the subject area. However, you are being assessed on your understanding of the concepts under consideration, so you need to be able to demonstrate your understanding by explaining theories before you use them. A good tip is to write as if the person who will read your work knows a little about the subject area, but not much, so you need to explain concepts fully for them. You can use textbooks to help you explain difficult concepts if you're experiencing difficulty expressing complex ideas in your own words, but try not to overuse quotations as this will only suggest that you don't really understand, and will also reduce your word limit. Quotations are usually not included in your word count, but if you have half a page of quotations, then you are in danger of not writing in such a way as to satisfy your tutor that you understand. Try to paraphrase from secondary sources, but remember that you will still need to acknowledge the source of your information.

Example 1

Here is an example from an essay written by a student who has been asked to explain how theoretical frameworks can help us to explain comic effects in plays. The extract she has chosen to illustrate her answer is from Willy Russell's *Educating Rita*. The model she is using is that of Grice's cooperative principle, which proposes four 'maxims' for explaining cooperation in conversation.

Student example

> The playwright seems to exploit Grice's maxims and use conversational implicature to create comic effect, by violating the maxim of manner in Grice's 'cooperative principal' (Carter and Simpson 1989, 281).

Comment

This statement needs 'tidying up' in a number of ways to make it more academically accurate. Firstly, the referencing is incorrect. She has referred to 'Grice', but Grice is not mentioned in the reference. The source acknowledged is a secondary source which summarizes the work of Grice, so she should have acknowledged *both* the primary source and the secondary source, Carter and Simpson's summary. Secondly, the spelling of 'principal' is incorrect in this sense: the correct terminology is 'principle'. Thirdly, as noted above, we can't assume that playwrights, authors and poets consciously exploit theory even if they are aware of them. Fourthly, using 'seems' makes the statement sound unsure. Try to avoid words that indicate uncertainty in your writing. Notice that merely by omitting 'seems' the statement sounds more authoritative:

> The playwright exploits Grice's maxims and uses conversational implicature to create comic effect, by violating the maxim of manner in Grice's 'cooperative principal' (Carter and Simpson 1989, 281).

However, a more accurate rewording would be something along the lines of:

> We can explain the comic effect created by this conversational exchange by applying the maxims of Grice's cooperative principle (1975; cited in Carter and Simpson 1989, 281).

Similarly, writing about the same extract, the student comments that 'Rita violates the quantity maxim'. Just as writers don't intentionally exploit or violate frameworks, it's advisable not to write about characters as if they are deliberately acting in accordance with an understanding of linguistic theory.

Example 2

In the example below, a different student is analysing an extract of text using the notion of 'schema theory'. This theoretical model refers to the background knowledge which is shared by people within the same cultural context. We make sense of events in fictional texts by drawing upon our knowledge of what happens in real life. Incidentally, 'schema theory' is a concept that originates from psychology, and demonstrates the links between humanities and science-based subjects (see section on originality).

Task – Make a note of the difference between this student's explanation of theory and the one above. Why is this student's more successful?

The text the student is analysing is from an episode of the sitcom *Friends*. In the episode under discussion, the student is analysing a conversation between best friends Rachel and Monica. Monica has been to lunch with Julie, her brother Ross's girlfriend. Rachel has a crush on Ross so Monica hasn't told her about seeing Julie in case it upsets her. When Rachel find out, the two women have an argument in which it becomes clear that Rachel feels betrayed, and the language used is that of a betrayed partner and a cheating spouse.

Student Example

> For most viewers, they would recognize such an argument as a stereotypical dispute that would occur between a couple, when one of them is caught cheating. This background knowledge is likely to be held in their schemas for affairs and unfaithfulness. It is interesting that most people would recognize the argument because of their background knowledge or schema, even though the majority will not have experienced this situation for themselves. Instead, the knowledge is likely to come from books, television, film and the media in general, since 'fictions play a large part in the establishment of our schemas' (Short 1996, 227).

Comment

Notice how the student doesn't make generalizations about the background knowledge held by viewers, but uses phrases such as 'most viewers', 'likely' and 'the majority', and her discussion is supported by a well-integrated quotation, correctly referenced. This is different from the uncertainty conveyed by the word 'seems' above. Her writing is authoritative without assuming that all viewers will respond in exactly the same way. The first sentence is a little 'clunky', and a more successful wording might have been, 'Most viewers would recognize …'. Try to organize your time so that you can leave essays for a day or so before submitting, as returning to your work with fresh eyes can help you to proofread and edit writing that previously looked fine.

Academic Tone: 'Talking the Talk'

Sounding authoritative

As with any other area of life, academic writing has its own 'jargon' and you will be more successful if you can adopt an appropriate academic tone. You will at some point in your academic career have looked at the difference between formal and informal language use. While you may have got away with a degree of informality in Year One (Level 4) your tutors will be expecting that to have largely disappeared at Level 5. The key to adopting an academic style of writing is by reading widely and thinking about the words used by authors of textbooks and journal articles. You don't need to use unfamiliar vocabulary to sound academic: clarity is more important. Often the difference between good academic writing and less successful writing is a hesitancy in style which is due to students' lack of confidence with the ideas they are putting across.

Consider the following example:

> I think Chomsky's argument that language is innate is probably more convincing than Halliday's functional approach.

Here the student is bringing together competing arguments and weighing them against one another (synthesizing) to make a judgement (evaluating). So far so good. Clearly the student has done what is expected of him at this level, but he doesn't sound very convinced. Compare the following:

> Chomsky's argument that language is innate is more convincing than Halliday's functional approach, for the following reasons.

By removing those features that indicate uncertainty ('I think', 'probably') the sentence now sounds more authoritative and convincing, especially as the student can now go on to summarize the arguments. This type of summary might appear as an introduction to a topic in order to 'signpost' to the reader the direction of the argument. We will return to 'signposting' later on.

The right words for the job

Sometimes, substituting a word or phrase can help to create a more successful academic tone. Your tutor will be expecting you to demonstrate your understanding of terminology by using it and applying it correctly, before going on to evaluate its usefulness. Avoid using words that don't really say anything, such as the following:

The use of alliteration makes the text flow.

'Flow' isn't a very effective term for describing texts. What does it actually mean? A quick look in an online dictionary will give you some possible synonyms. 'Movement' came up when I did a Google search: 'A steady, continuous stream or supply of something'. Sometimes students use the term 'flow' when they are trying to describe the way a text's structure makes us read more quickly, or the ways in which the text is constructed to encourage the reader to make sense of the way in which ideas have been linked together.

In the first instance, you would need to explain what it is about the construction of the text that creates that effect. It might be a predominance of conjunctions, or shorter words: or a greater use of dynamic verbs which create an impression of movement. Alternatively, it might be due to cohesive features: words that belong to the same or similar semantic fields, or use of extended metaphors. Think about the effect you are trying to explain.

Returning to our example above, we could perhaps now reword 'The use of alliteration makes the text flow' by substituting 'movement'. To illustrate this, here's an example from the nursery rhyme 'Hickory Dickory Dock':

Hickory dickory dock,

The mouse ran up the clock.

The clock struck one,

The mouse ran down,

Hickory dickory dock.

If you look again at our sentence, 'The use of alliteration makes the text flow', it doesn't really explain what's happening. But if we now use our synonym 'movement', we might be getting somewhere: 'The use of dynamic verbs such as "ran and struck", together with the deictic features "up" and "down" produce a sense of movement.' Now consider the sentence structure and length, the rhyme and half-rhyme, and the sequencing of events. How might we use these to reinforce the analysis?

'Signposting' Your Argument

Imagine you're visiting a town for the first time. You know where you want to go but aren't sure how you're going to get there. You would be a bit disconcerted if there were no signs to help you to find your way. Writing a good academic essay depends on letting your reader know the 'route' through your argument to your conclusions. If you look at a journal article, it will be clearly signposted: the abstract will summarize the journey, and section headings will help you to follow the direction of the argument. Presumably you've followed the correct route through this book to reach this point! Although sometimes section headings are encouraged in certain types of writing, there are times when they are not expected. However you still need to help your reader to follow the organization of your argument. It might be as simple as using the following discourse markers:

Firstly …

Secondly …

Finally …

Or:

On the one hand …

On the other hand …

In conclusion …

Other ways of signposting are:

In addition …

Alternatively …

By contrast …

However …

Similarly …

In conclusion …

Introductions, Summaries, Abstracts and Essay Titles

The way in which you organize your writing into logical sections is an important way of guiding your reader through your argument. I advise my students to write in sections, especially for longer pieces of work such as extended projects or dissertations. Trying to write in a linear fashion often isn't the most effective method as you can lose yourself in your argument, and if you're lost then your reader has no chance! There are different ways of doing this and everyone has their preferred method. You could work in sections in one long document, or keep separate files with different names and put them together later. Some students keep an online blog from which they can cut and paste (you can set the privacy settings if you don't want anyone else to read it!). By working in this way you can organize your work into paragraphs that follow a logical order. Introductions are a way of signposting and these are often the hardest to write. I usually tell my students to write introductions last as it's easier to explain the purpose and direction of your essay once you've written it! You may be required to write an abstract summarizing your work so that others will be able to understand what you have done, and have an indication of your findings and your conclusion. If you have been able to choose your own topic, then the title of your assignment should indicate what you are going to write about. These sorts of skills are often the hardest to master, so it's worth pausing occasionally to summarize for yourself what it is you are actually trying to achieve and whether you have drifted off topic.

If you can signpost your argument in this way, not only will you signal to your reader that you are 'steering' them in the right direction, it will also help you to remain focused. Plus, it may help you to demonstrate those Level 5 skills of synthesizing and evaluating competing and complex arguments and reaching a conclusion.

Here is an example of signposting from a student's essay.

Task – Make a note of the signposting features. How successful is this student in enabling us to follow her argument?

> The three advertisements chosen for semiotic analysis are as follows: Figure 1 demonstrates a poster from 1970 used to advertise 'Mr Legg slacks'. Figure 2 is an image chosen from a photo shoot published in *Vogue Italia* in 2006, which was photographed by Steven Meisel, whose work depicts fashion in a controversial way. And finally, Figure 3 is an advert for the Italian fashion designers Dolce and Gabbana, published in the Spanish issue of the magazine *Esquire* in 2007. A semiotic analysis of these images allows the paradigmatic and syntagmatic choices made by the photographers and designers to be examined. Furthermore, an understanding of these choices as well as other factors such as anchorage and relay enable one to study the effects these elements will have on the target audience.

Comment

The student first outlines the adverts she is going to analyse in order, with some discussion of context before describing the direction of her argument. You might have noted her use of 'as follows', 'Figure 1', 'Figure 2', 'And finally, Figure 3' and 'Furthermore', before telling us how these images will be used in her analysis.

Below is an extract from a student's exam answer to the following question:

> Culpeper (1998, 83) argues that the notion of 'face' and 'politeness' are particularly useful in the study of drama.
>
> In light of this argument, explain the relationship between the two. How far do you agree with Culpeper's view?

What follows is her introduction. This student went on to produce a thorough answer for which she received a high 2:1.

Task – Try to identify the features that made her answer so successful.

> The relationship between face and politeness can be explained by the fact that 'the difference between politeness and impoliteness is (the hearer's interpretation of) intention'; whether the speaker intends to support face (politeness) or 'attack' it (impoliteness) (Culpeper 1998). Therefore politeness and face are two concepts that are closely linked, since if one supports face, he/she is being polite and vice versa. To fully understand this, the concept of 'face' must firstly be defined. According to Brown and Levinson (1978) face is 'the public self-image every member wants for himself'. Therefore face is the way a person is portrayed to everyone else. This concept can be further split into two: positive face, which is the 'positive and consistent self image people have of themselves' (Brown and Levinson 1978), and is therefore our desire to be liked and approved of; in contrast, negative face can be defined as 'the want of every competent adult member of a culture to have his or her actions unimpeded by others' (Culrone 2011). Therefore the relationship between politeness and face can be seen through an example of paying a compliment (e.g., 'You look nice'), which supports a person's positive face and is therefore polite. In contrast, commanding someone to do something attacks their negative face (e.g., 'Get out of my house now!') and is, in turn, impolite. The usefulness of the two concepts can be seen in the fact that Leech (1983) states 'politeness overrides all other conversational behaviour'.

How to Analyse the Language of a Text: An Example

As we read through a text for the first time we are responding intuitively to the language used. As a student of language you need to be able to discuss how the language used has achieved this effect on you. In your first year you will have examined linguistic features and categorized them correctly. At this level your analysis needs to be more sophisticated and detailed.

The following extract is taken from a recipe book based on a popular cookery series on TV. It is the introduction to a section on chocolate.

Task – Read through the text a few times and underline any features that are particularly noticeable (foregrounded) for you. Once you've done that, consider contextual features: Who is the text written for and how do you know? What purpose is the writer trying to achieve? Consider genre conventions: How does it compare with the conventions of a more traditional recipe? Is there anything here that is characteristic of Slater's writing style, or that of other cookery writers? Can you make any links to wider social/cultural factors? Once you've made detailed notes, compare what you have written with my comments below.

Remember, my analysis is not exhaustive, but I've considered how the language used creates an effect and linked it to social and cultural context. How does your analysis compare? Are there any similarities or differences? All interpretation is subjective, and it may be that you have noted features that I haven't commented on or have a different interpretation. If you have supported your analysis with appropriate and accurate examples from the text, then there isn't any reason why your interpretation should be incorrect.

> Dark and velvety sauces; smooth mild ice creams; warming soporific drinks and sugar-laden fudge. Chocolate runs through my life like a comfort blanket; a teddy bear you can eat. I can show off with boxes of truffles from the most expensive Parisian shops or devour a Toffee Crisp in absolute solitude. For all my banging on about the world's finest chocolate, I can still demolish a packet of Rolos in minutes. I simply love chocolate. I adore it. I want it. (Nigel Slater, *Real Food*, 1998)

The first impression I noted was the listing effect of the first sentence and the sounds of the words which seem symbolic of melted chocolate – 'velvety', 'sauces', 'smooth', 'warming', 'soporific'. This effect seems to be partly achieved by the long vowel sounds – 'au' in sauce, 'oo' in 'smooth', 'ar' in warming – and partly due to the sibilance in 'sauces', 'smooth' and 'ice creams', which causes the reader to linger over the words. Although the words are not sound symbolic in the traditional sense, it may be that we make symbolic associations between the length of time it takes to read the words with the length of time it might take to pour a sauce or to drink a hot chocolate. This is reinforced by the metaphor 'runs' in 'chocolate runs through my life'. I noted the number of adjectives – there are seven in the first sentence alone, and some are quite sophisticated – 'sugar-laden', 'soporific'. 'Sugar-laden' could be seen as a negative adjective in our health-conscious society, but the writer also alludes to childish treats – 'comfort blanket', 'teddy bear' – and sweets associated with childhood – 'Rolos', 'Toffee Crisp' – which suggests the innocent pleasure children take in sweets that might be deemed unhealthy by weight-conscious adults. Some of the verbs used to describe eating also have connotations of child-like or animal-like behaviour – 'devour', 'demolish'. There is a contrast therefore between the more sophisticated associations – 'dark and velvety sauces', 'boxes of truffles', 'expensive Parisian shops', 'world's finest chocolate' – and the 'Rolos' and 'Toffee Crisp', which implies chocolate is versatile and appealing to all ages. The writer also makes use of a superlative – 'the most expensive' – to make the contrast more explicit. Similarly, his use of the adjective 'absolute' to premodify 'solitude' is interesting – 'absolute solitude' is in contrast to 'show off', and illustrates the difference between expensive chocolate and cheaper chocolate bars: one is for display as well as pleasure, the other is simply for pleasure. It might also be worth noting that the target audience (presumably adults who like to cook) is assumed to already have knowledge of the types of sweets described and may be culturally specific, as sweets often have different names, or are unknown to people from other countries.

There is an extended metaphor in the second sentence, beginning with the simile 'like a comfort blanket', and continuing with the metaphor 'a teddy bear you can eat'. The register is informal but there is a mixture of complex vocabulary – 'soporific' – and an informal, conversational/colloquial tone – 'banging on', 'show off' – which seems to address an educated adult audience, in keeping with the style of his TV programmes on the BBC early on Friday evenings.

There is a three-part list at the end of the extract containing stative verbs which are almost synonymous – 'love' and 'adore' are in the same area of meaning, but 'adore' refers to a stronger emotion than does 'love'. 'Want' is in the semantic area of desire, which again relates to strong emotion. These three sentences are also short in comparison with the remainder of the text, creating a foregrounding effect which acts as a climax to what has gone before.

Slater's prose is descriptive and full of imagery which is almost poetic, which might be deemed unusual in a recipe book. However, there is an increasing tendency for cookery writers to attract their audience by including additional information as well as recipes, presumably in an attempt to persuade readers to purchase their books in the face of competition from others – for example, Delia Smith, Nigella Lawson and Jamie Oliver, to name just three. There has also been a rise in the popularity of cookery programmes in contemporary society, which requires writers to be able to attract more readers and viewers in a fiercely competitive market. Although this text was written in 1998, the fact that Slater is still attracting viewers suggests the success of his use of language.

I hope this chapter has helped you with your second year of study. See you in Year Three!

ENGLISH LANGUAGE: YEAR THREE
Val Jessop

Introduction

This chapter will enable you to monitor your own progress in the final year. It discusses how you can become an even more independent student, as well as giving advice on how to prepare for, and write, your dissertation. Some guidance will be given as to the pitfalls of research topics and how to avoid these. You will also be shown examples of extracts from high-achieving students in an effort to demonstrate how you too can be successful in your final year.

Welcome

Congratulations – you've made it to Year Three! By now you will not only have acquired the skills and knowledges you need for studying English language at undergraduate level, you will have also learned how to synthesize and evaluate complex ideas and come to a conclusion about their respective merits. These are 'transferable' skills that are sought after by employers, as they demonstrate your ability to appreciate and assess the merits of alternative viewpoints and come to your own conclusions. Now that you have reached Level 6, your tutors will be assessing your ability not only to do all of those things but to be critical of the ideas you come across. This doesn't mean being critical in the everyday sense of the term, but is the ability to question and critique ideas, to assess strengths and weaknesses in arguments and to generate new ideas from previous research. This latter part is particularly relevant when it comes to the final honours dissertation, the piece of work that students often worry about most.

Monitoring Your Progress

By this stage, you should be aware of your academic progress to date: your strengths and areas that you still need to improve, whether you perform better in exams or coursework, and the marks you are capable of achieving. Continue to develop your strengths by looking at the feedback given to you by tutors. Sometimes students feel that because they have achieved a good mark they don't need to read all of the tutor's comments on their work, but it's important to know what has been rewarded so that you can build on that in future work. On the other hand, a lower mark can have a demoralizing effect, and you may not want to read the feedback. It's important to realize that a low mark is not intended as a judgement on you personally but on what you've submitted – the tutor can only assess what's there in front of them. Any comments should direct you to something that needs attention in your work, so force yourself to read what your tutor has written to make sure you don't make the same mistakes again. Write notes to yourself to remind you if errors are recurring. If you're unsure of why you've received a low mark (or indeed a high one) ask your tutor for clarification.

Task – Look back at two pieces of work and compare the feedback. Are you making any of the same mistakes? How can you respond to that in your next piece of work?

Becoming Independent

There are many demands on your time and deadlines will soon loom large. Many of these may be set around the same time. You will of course have already experienced this, but on top of that you now have your dissertation to worry about. Many students put that off in favour of meeting deadlines that appear more pressing because they're more imminent. It's a good idea at the beginning of the year to timetable periods for yourself where you can work on your dissertation, because leaving it until the last minute is a sure way of producing a substandard piece of work. If you can get into the habit of planning your study timetable so that you know when your deadlines are and how you will fit in this substantial amount of research and writing, and stick to it, then you may also find that you can timetable some time to just relax and/or have fun! You may also be having to submit application forms for jobs or further courses and attending interviews and/ or doing work experience, and all of these commitments will have to be balanced with time for completing essays and doing exams. Independent research requires a great deal of time and a dissertation isn't something that can be rushed at the last minute, so it's important to be organized to avoid a last minute panic as the final deadline approaches. We will return to the dissertation later. Another change in the third year is that you may also find you're offered more freedom in the choice of topics that you're being assessed on, or even the way in which you are assessed. This is all part of becoming able to solve problems independently, one of the transferable skills discussed earlier.

Being Original

In the previous chapter, I suggested that you make yourself familiar with the marking criteria against which your work is being assessed. One of these may relate to originality, and I touched on this in my discussion of revision tips above. The marking criteria used for assessing students' work on my course is divided into six elements: 'relevance', 'knowledge', 'analysis', 'argument and structure', 'originality' and 'presentation'. Take a look at the marking criteria for 'originality': the student's work is graded depending on the description which best fits the standard of submission:

> Distinctive work showing independent thought and critical engagement with alternative views.

This is the description of work which falls into the 'first class' (1st) category. Notice how the wording changes as we work down the levels:

> May contain some distinctive or independent thinking: may begin to formulate an independent position. (2:1)

> Sound work which expresses a personal position only in broad terms and in uncritical conformity to one or more standard views of the topic. (2:2)

> Largely derivative; no personal view is adequately formulated. (3rd)

Notice that the key terms are 'distinctive', 'independent' and 'critical engagement'. You need to have enough time to read around your topic in depth, read what's been written from alternative viewpoints, and have critiqued those views. If any of those elements are missing from your work, then you won't be able to achieve at the higher levels. So you need to learn to be able to express your own opinion, synthesize similar and opposing views, and evaluate and critique those views. Each of these terms will be explained further on.

Finding Your Own Voice

This is one of the things most students find very difficult. Now that you are in your final year, not only are you expected to have acquired an academic style of writing, you need to be able to express your own opinion in a way that doesn't sound opinionated. In other words, you need to be able to express your own views in a manner which demonstrates that you have researched a topic thoroughly, evaluated the evidence for and against an argument, and can critique those arguments before expressing your own conclusion based on all of the above. If you examine the learning outcomes against which your work is being assessed you will probably see terms such as 'evaluate', 'synthesize', 'critique', 'analyse' or even 'critically evaluate'. If you aren't able to do these things you won't be able to achieve the learning outcomes.

Evaluating and Critiquing

These terms don't mean saying a piece of research or secondary reading is 'wrong' or 'disproved'. By evaluating and critiquing someone's work you are looking for its strengths, and for areas that have been disputed by other critics or theorists, or for cases where the argument isn't supported by alternative research. It's very bad practice to criticize the work of someone else in the normal sense of the word. A critique demonstrates your ability to weigh up the pros and cons of an argument and come to a conclusion based on the evidence. At this level, you are expected to demonstrate independent thinking, so it's even more important to read widely and find underexplored areas of research.

Synthesis

At Level 5 you are expected to make links between different areas and combine them into a strong and convincing argument. Look for themes – critics discussing the same topic area – then look for common elements of agreement. Needless to say this is a skill that can only be developed if you read widely. Superficial reading around the topic will show itself in a 'thin' essay, which could be evident from its inability to meet the word count. As you begin to identify areas that are agreed upon by a number of critics, you should also find others who have a different viewpoint or explanation, especially if you have broadened your reading into different disciplines. You will already have been expected to evaluate opposing views at Level 5, but now you need to think in more detail about why these opposing ideas have arisen (i.e., 'critically evaluate'). Is there an inherent weakness in the argument(s) put forward, an unexplored gap or an alternative explanation, for example? It might be a good idea to see if your library has unpublished doctoral theses that you can borrow for ideas, as PhD students have to explore areas for original research. Remember to acknowledge these sources in the same way as any other secondary source. Journal articles are also a good resource so check for collections in the library.

Below is an extract from a student's exam answer to a question about the effect of computer-mediated communication on social relationships.

Task – Read the example below. Is it a successful example of 'synthesis'? Make a few notes as to why you think it is / is not a good example.

Example from a student's exam answer

> One person who views computer-mediated communication as having negative effects on face-to-face communication, Krauti, suggests that computer-mediated communication causes a reduction in the size of a person's real-life social circle, and an increase in depression and loneliness. Kujath also makes a similar claim, saying that the use of computer-mediated communication results in 'deteriorating relationship quality and decreased intimacy among its users' (Kujath 2011). Thus, these two critics are positing dystopian views of the Internet as a tool for communication.
>
> Conversely, Bargh and McKenna suggest that the use of computer-mediated communication can actually help a person to maintain existing relations, and help the formation of new relationships. Ellison extends this viewpoint by suggesting that most 'friendships' on a social networking site have a real-life background. Lampe also holds this opinion, saying that in a study of college students, he found that people are more likely to use social networking sites to contact people who they have already met in real life rather than to contact strangers. Thus these critics are showing a 'utopian' attitude towards the use of the Internet for communication purposes.

Comment

This is a good example of synthesis; the student has summarized views from a number of sources and identified two opposing views, and she has supported her answer with integrated quotations. You may notice that she hasn't included dates for some of her sources: this can be overlooked in an exam answer, as it is clear that she has read widely around the topic area. She has also produced a critique of the work she has cited, by arguing that one view is more convincing than another, and uses this to form the conclusion.

Overall, it can be stated that if computer-mediated communication is used alongside face-to-face communication, as discussed by Lampe, then social networking sites can be seen in a utopian light, as they help to maintain existing relations, and to formulate new ones.

Writing the Dissertation: Why Do We Make You Do This?

It's worth explaining a little bit about why the dissertation is so important. Earlier I discussed the fact that all institutions who deliver higher education programmes have to comply with a 'quality code' set by the Quality Assurance Agency. Students graduating with a degree in English should have acquired comparable skills and achieved to the same level. These standards are underpinned by 'subject benchmark statements', which describe the skills that English graduates are expected to have at the end of their programme of study. Some of these statements refer to subject knowledge, and some to transferable skills: skills that employers are looking for in potential employees such as problem solving, time management and an ability to work independently.

A dissertation allows you to demonstrate your awareness of relevant research into language and of its complexity, as well as enabling you to show skills of independent study, development of a logical and coherent argument, evaluation and critique. You will also be expected to demonstrate these skills in other academic work of course, and it may be the case that your institution doesn't require you to produce an extended piece of work such as a lengthy dissertation. But a dissertation is an excellent opportunity to conduct some research into an area you are interested in and haven't been able to study in depth on your course, so don't be daunted by it. It requires good time management and organizational skills though, so it's worth being prepared for this earlier rather than later.

As part of your honours dissertation you will probably be expected to produce an overview of relevant research into your field of study. Before you can do that, you obviously need to decide what you want to research, which is often not as easy as it sounds.

Alternatives to the Dissertation

It may be that your institution is one of those that is looking at more creative methods of assessing Level 6 work. Those important skills of independent learning, time management and organizational skills can be assessed equally well in the form of portfolios or collections of essays on an academic topic.

Other examples might include an investigation into a research area that is presented digitally; an extended project or collaborative work; or written material undertaken on behalf of another institution, such as handbooks or other nonfiction to be used by volunteers, other students or in the workplace. Such examples offer similar challenges and problem-solving skills to the traditional dissertation, but have an advantage in that they might culminate in a product which can be shown to potential employers.

The Dissertation: Deciding on Your Topic

This is probably one of the things that students find most difficult. You've spent the last two years answering questions set by your tutors and now you have to decide on your own. Many students get into difficulties because they don't focus on a topic early enough and don't leave themselves time to complete a successful research project. Some students end up deciding on a topic and then realize that they can't find enough background reading in that area, or that in fact they're bored with their topic. You have to live with your dissertation for a long time and write extensively on your topic, so it's worth focusing early to make sure you don't end up hating it! It's also a good idea to write down any ideas that occur to you as you go though Year Two as they may germinate into a research idea for the Year Three. You may have written notes for an essay that you didn't use because they weren't relevant to the question, for example. In other words, don't throw anything away. Keep a notebook of potential topics and revisit them.

Think about areas that you are particularly interested in but which haven't been covered in detail in your modules. Avoid broad areas: for example, students will say they want to look at bilingualism, or Shakespeare in schools, or animal communication. These are areas that require access to participants who are bilingual in the first example, and permission to go into a school in the second, which often poses difficulties. The third example is an area that has been covered extensively in literature about the subject, so it would be difficult to find an original area to research. Try to think about what it is specifically about the subject area that interests you and start small rather than thinking in generalizations. Ask if your library keeps copies of previous undergraduate dissertations. They may have suggestions for further research in their conclusion.

Writing the Literature Review

If you've found your focus, you will find writing the literature review easier than if you are thinking about a general topic area. The literature review summarizes the findings from your background reading and identifies any areas of disagreement, weaknesses or unexplored areas that might guide your research. It should not just be a list of books that you've read, but should direct your supervisor to your proposal for a research topic. If you've written it well, your supervisor will be able to give you feedback and ideas for writing the dissertation itself. If you don't write a successful literature review then you won't receive the most useful advice, as your supervisor won't know which direction your research is heading in or what you want to find out. Another advantage is that if you've done this part successfully, you should be able to incorporate the review into your dissertation. If you haven't focused early enough, then you won't be able to do this.

Conducting Empirical Research (Primary Research)

You may decide you want to go out and collect research data of your own to replicate a study you've read or to conduct similar research with a different group of participants. You may have a research question that you want to answer, or you may want to test a hypothesis. In the former, you won't know what you are going to find out; in the latter, you may have an assumption that you want to test. An example of a research question might be something like 'Do girls and boys use language differently when playing with children of the same sex?' Formulated as a hypothesis, it might read: 'Girls use co-operative language with girls, but boys dominate in mixed sex groups.'

It's important to remember that this kind of research is time consuming, both in terms of collecting data and writing up your findings. However it has the advantage of making your dissertation original, as no one else will have exactly the same results. You will need to ask yourself some questions before you embark on this kind of research however, for example, whether you will be able to access your participants. Students sometimes decide they want to conduct primary research into child language acquisition for example, so the first question I ask is whether they know any young children. Any research involving children or vulnerable people will raise questions about ethics, especially if those participants are not related to you personally.

Other students might decide they want to look at educational issues within schools: i.e., comparing the language used by children from different backgrounds. This is another minefield, as schools may be wary of your findings, and obtaining permission is often very difficult. You need to think very carefully therefore about whether the type of primary research you want to conduct is feasible.

Ethical Issues

If you are conducting primary research, it is likely that your institution will require you to consider carefully any ethical issues, some of which have been indicated above. Any research involving children or vulnerable adults, anything that might be connected with ethnicity, sexual orientation or religion are areas that are probably better avoided. You may find that you have put a great deal of work into a proposal that is rejected on the grounds that it is not ethical and you will have to think again. It's worth seeking advice early on about whether your proposal is viable to avoid wasting time on something that you can't continue.

Keeping Accurate Records

Once you have decided on your research area, it's important to make accurate notes to avoid the heartache of losing data or references later on. With empirical research, if you are recording interviews or taking videos, make sure your equipment is working properly before you begin. I can remember recording a particularly interesting interview, only to realize I'd pressed 'play' on the recorder instead of 'record', so most of that data was lost. If you're recording more than one person, think about any additional noise in the room. It's very time consuming having to listen to recordings over and over again because you can't make out what people are saying. Make notes on the context of any recordings: the time of day, the surroundings, whether or not the setting is familiar to the participants, whether you know them well or not at all – all of these are factors that can affect the way that people behave.

It's not just primary data that needs to be recorded accurately however. Every time you read a book, make sure you keep an accurate record of all the relevant information – title, authors, dates and most importantly page numbers. If you have a really useful quotation but can't remember where it's from, then you can't use it, and the chances of finding it again are probably remote. Organize your notes as you go along so that you can start to see themes and trends; for example, 'Problems with X's Linguistic Framework' or 'Strengths of X's Linguistic Framework'. You'll find this more useful than general headings. Get into the habit of keeping a notebook with you at all times, as you never know when a good idea will occur to you.

Don't Put Off Writing

I've lost count of the number of students who tell me that they're getting on with the research but haven't yet started writing. It's much better to write as you go along, so set yourself small targets that will give you a sense of achievement. There's no need to start at the beginning and keep writing. In fact, the introduction is probably the last thing you will write. Once you've read something, write up a summary of that reading and your own thoughts about it. You may not use it in the end, but then again you might, and it will save time in the long run. Don't worry about being formal or having correct punctuation at this stage, and ignore any typing errors. It's more important just to record your ideas, and it's more satisfying than deciding you're 'going to work on the dissertation'. As you type up your notes, start to structure them into topic areas or themes – use headings or separate documents and keep a backup. You can find storage space on the Internet to upload your documents, so that if your computer crashes or you lose your memory stick you can still access your work online. Dropbox is a useful one and some e-mail clients also allow you to store files. You could even keep your notes in the form of a blog; some students find this more enjoyable, and you can copy and paste them into a more formal document once you're done. If you write continuously as you're going along, you'll find you've soon reached your word count, and the final draft won't feel quite so daunting.

Making the Most of Supervision Meetings

Make sure you are fully prepared when you meet with your supervisor. Because this is a piece of independent research, you will be limited to the number of appointments you have with your tutor, so you need to make the most of them. It may also be up to you to ask for an appointment as, depending on the institution, your supervisors won't necessarily be chasing you to see where you're up to, so don't put off seeing them until you've left it too late. Planning your supervision meetings is part of the process of independent study, as is knowing when you can work on your own, and when you need some direction. Supervision meetings allow you to discuss your work in progress, and it is just that – it doesn't need to be perfect before you meet with your supervisor. However, it's also not a good idea to turn up for an appointment without knowing exactly what you want to research or what you want to ask. Have a list of questions you want to ask as well as a summary of your findings to date if you have any, or at least a summary of secondary research and any questions it has generated for you. This will help your supervisor to help you. It's very difficult to give advice to someone who doesn't really know what they want. Regular supervision meetings enable your supervisor to see your work in progress, so make sure you use them!

Example from an Undergraduate Dissertation

This is an extract from an undergraduate dissertation into the language of informational leaflets for prospective parents. The student wanted to explore the way in which the leaflets attempt to persuade people to stop smoking if they are pregnant, and encourage a no-smoking policy in the home. This extract is from his review of relevant research.

Task – Read the extract. Do you think this student is critiquing?

> Van Dijk (1998) argues that ideology does not purely denote a system of beliefs; on the contrary, they are belief systems shared within the framework of society (1998, 135). It can be inferred from Van Dijk's argument that for an ideology to achieve its purpose, it must have its beliefs accepted by those within society, therefore indicating that within society there is resistance to the ideological belief systems of the dominant social groups. According to Althusser, 'the existence of ideology and the hailing or interpellating of individuals as subjects is one and the same thing' (1971, 49). However, it can be argued that for interpellation to be effective the intended target audience has to respond to the 'hailing'.
>
> Althusser (1968) argues that the transmission of ideology within society takes place by the use of ideological state apparatuses and repressive state apparatuses. The ideological state apparatus refers to institutions that transmit religious or educational views, whereas repressive state apparatuses refer to the police, thus alluding to rule by force (1968, 296–7). However, Althusser's argument fails to account for the transmission of power relations within society via the subjects of the state. If the example of health literature successfully interpellates the subject into an idealized position, then not only will they give up smoking, additionally they will begin to monitor the behaviours of others. An example of this can be demonstrated by the subject accepting the ideology of a 'smoke-free home', thus once this is fully achieved any attempt to smoke in the home would be perceived as a threat.

Comment

The student has clearly summarized the theoretical frameworks he is using: it would be fairly easy for an educated reader to understand these ideas even if he or she hadn't come across them before. His writing illustrates the way in which you shouldn't assume the reader is your tutor or is someone who already knows about your topic (even though in reality it will be). By doing this, the student has demonstrated his understanding. He has also produced a critique: notice he comments that 'Althusser's argument fails to account for ...' and goes on to provide an original example – in this case, literature relating to health issues. He also makes links to the wider social context and power relationships in contemporary society. Originality is evident in that he has taken some established ideas from Althusser's writing in the sixties and seventies, referred to more recent work, and applied those ideas to his own experience as a prospective father reading health literature for today's prospective parents.

The Last Hurdle

You've finished writing the body of your dissertation and are feeling like a huge weight has been lifted from your shoulders. Don't forget to leave yourself time to proofread (although hopefully you've been doing this as you went along). Check all your references are there, and everything you've acknowledged is in your bibliography. Check that you have complied with any requirements about margins, depths of headers and footers, page numbering, binding, etc. as some institutions are very picky about the format of dissertations and want them to conform to a standard. Most important, make sure you've left enough time to print it out, especially if you are expected to submit more than one copy. It's probably better to check with a printing firm as this may be more cost-effective. Do check well in advance how much notice they require though, as the last thing you want is to work up until the last minute and risk missing the deadline because it can't be printed in time!

Destinations

The nature of our discipline means that graduates from English degrees tend to have more opportunities for entering a wide range of career paths. Some graduates may choose to extend their knowledge of a particular area by pursuing a course at postgraduate level. Others may want to take a teacher training programme in order to enter careers in adult education or teaching in primary or secondary schools. If this is your goal then you should aim to obtain work experience early in the area of education that you anticipate you want to enter. There are a wide range of employment opportunities for graduates with the highly developed communicative skills which an English degree can develop. You might be interested in careers in the public services for example, or in professional roles within business and management, or community, social and personal services, or the retail trade, or within the police and justice services.

Being able to problem solve, to communicate effectively with people from different backgrounds and within a wide range of contexts, and having a high level of literacy make an English graduate an attractive prospect for employers, and some companies offer 'fast track' programmes to graduates. If you aren't sure exactly what you want to do after finishing your degree, make sure you attend any graduate and/or employment fairs on offer and talk to potential employers and careers advisors.

Goodbye and Good Luck

You've spent the last few years meeting strict deadlines, juggling assignments and work and/or family commitments and suddenly it's all over! Some students feel a sense of anticlimax: you've probably made some great friends and the university has become a sort of home from home, so it's not surprising if you feel a sense of loss at the end. Make sure you've made some plans – have a well-deserved holiday, visit friends or read a book because you want to, not because you have to! Most of all, congratulate yourself on completing your course – it's a huge achievement. Well done and good luck for the future!

BIBLIOGRAPHY

Year One

Cameron, D. 2012. *Verbal Hygiene*. London: Routledge.

Chandler, D. 2007 *Semiotics: The Basics*. London: Routledge.

Croft, W., and D. Cruse. 2004. *Cognitive Linguistics*. Cambridge: Cambridge University Press.

Crystal, D. 2004. *Rediscover Grammar*. London: Longman.

_____. 2005. *The Stories of English*. London: Longman.

_____. 2007. *How Language Works*. London: Penguin.

Fairclough, N. 1989. *Language and Power*. London: Routledge.

Fillmore, C. 2006. *Form and Meaning in Language*. Chicago: University of Chicago Press.

Fowler, R. 1991. *Language in the News: Discourse and Ideology in the Press*. London: Routledge.

_____. 1996. *Linguistic Criticism*. Oxford: Oxford Paperbacks.

Holmes, J. 2013. *An Introduction to Sociolinguistics*. London: Routledge.

Jeffries, L. 2009. *Critical Stylistics: The Power of English*. London: Palgrave Macmillan.

Lakoff, G., and M. Johnson. 2003. *Metaphors We Live By*. Chicago: University of Chicago Press.

Leech, G. 1973. *A Linguistic Guide to English Poetry*. London: Routledge.

_____. 1981. *Style in Fiction*. London: Routledge.

Short, M. 1996. *Exploring the Language of Poems, Plays and Prose*. London: Routledge.

Further resources:

Cross Disciplinary Approaches to Critical Discourse Analysis (CADAAD)

Poetics and Linguistics Association (PALA)

Cambridge Journal of Linguistics

Studies in Language

Modern Language Journal

Journal of Pragmatics

Phonetica

Linguistic Review

Year Two

Slater, N. 1998. *Real Food*. London: Fourth Estate.

The following are useful texts for explaining and exploring terms used in language analysis and stylistics in a range of literary and non-literary texts:

Carter, R., A. Goddard, D. Reah et al. 1997. *Working with Texts*. London: Routledge.

Culpeper, J., M. Short and P. Verdonk, eds. 1998. *Exploring the Language of Drama: From Text to Context*. London: Routledge.

Jeffries, L., and D. McIntyre. 2010. *Stylistics*. Cambridge: Cambridge University Press.

Short, M. 1996. *Exploring the Language of Poems, Plays and Prose*. London: Longman.

Toolan, M. 1992. *Language, Text and Context: Essays in Stylistics*. London: Routledge.

For a developmental approach to areas in stylistics, this resource book enables you to follow a particular theme through increasingly sophisticated examples:

Simpson, P. 2004. *Stylistics: A Resource Book for Students*. London: Routledge.

For learning about language in use, the following are helpful:

Cameron, D. 2001. *Working with Spoken Discourse*. London: Sage.

Thomas, J. 1995. *Meaning in Interaction*. Longman.

Wardaugh, R. 1986. *How Conversation Works*. London: Routledge.

For general texts on sociolinguistics try:

Holmes, J. 2000. *An Introduction to Sociolinguistics*. Oxford: Oxford University Press.

Milroy, L., and M. Gordon. 2003. *Sociolinguistics: Method and Interpretation*. Oxford: Blackwell.

Trudgill, P. 2000. *Sociolinguistics: An Introduction to Language and Society*. London: Penguin.

For help with using semiotic analysis try:

Chandler, D. 2002. *Semiotics: The Basics*. London: Routledge.

Fiske, J. 1982. *Introduction to Communication Studies*. London: Routledge.

Goodman, S., and D. Graddoll. 1996. *Redesigning English: New Texts, New Identities*. London: Routledge.

Jeffries, L. 1998. *Meaning in English*. London: Macmillan.

Kress, G., and T. van Leeuwen. 1996. *Reading Images: The Grammar of Visual Design*. London: Routledge.

For a full list of unintentionally ambiguous headlines:

ALTA (Australasian Language Technology Association). 2013. 'Humorous (but Real) Newspaper Headlines'. Online: http://www.alta.asn.au/events/altss_w2003_proc/altss/courses/somers/headlines.htm (accessed 9 May 2014).

Year Three

Jeffries, L. 2010. *Critical Stylistics: The Power of English*. London: Palgrave Macmillan.

Lambrou, M., and P. Stockwell. 2007. *Contemporary Stylistics*. London: Continuum.

For help with writing your dissertation:

Cottrell, S. 2005. *Critical Thinking Skills: Developing Effective Analysis and Argument*. Hants: Palgrave.

Cottrell, S., and C. Hart. 1998. *Doing a Literature Review*. London: Sage.

Rudestan, E, and R. N. Newton. 2000. *Surviving your Dissertation: A Comprehensive Guide to Content and Process*. London: Sage.

Silverman, D. 2001. *Interpreting Qualitative Data: Methods for Analyzing Talk, Text and Interaction*. London: Sage.

Part Two
English Literature

ENGLISH LITERATURE: YEAR ONE
Devon Campbell-Hall

Introduction

This chapter tells you what to expect from your English literature degree. I ask the question, what is literature? and consider why we study literature at degree level, as well as what careers you can go on to after completion. I look at how you can prepare for study, how to progress from A-level to degree and the difficulties of coping as a mature student. I consider the various types of teaching you'll be introduced to and suggest how you can gain the most from them. In addition, I look at how best to take notes for your particular learner type, as well as assessments and how to structure your essays. We will also look at what learning outcomes are and how you can best prepare for exams. Crucially, we demystify the marking criteria. I also ask that all-important question: does the first year really count? All of this is spliced with handy advice from students and helpful exercises designed to make you think.

What Is Literature?

Studying English at uni these days is about reading and discussing the classics along with new and exciting types of literature. I have been able to chase my passion for hip hop, which is the subject I based my dissertation around – comparing it to World War One and Romantic poetry. This had a knock-on effect on my dream of being a teacher, as this freedom of study allowed me to express and further my interest in different types of literature, which is vital to reach all students from various backgrounds.

(Steve, graduate, BA (Hons) English and Media; just landed his dream job as a secondary English teacher at his former school)

By the end of this section, you should have some idea of:

- the origins of English literature as an academic discipline

- why literature is studied at university level

- the academic and transferable skills students can achieve on such a course

- the vocational and postgraduate opportunities available to students after graduation

- the difference between a linguistic and a literary analysis

- what is required of a literature analysis

The texts analysed on English degrees have always included the cherished trinity of poetry, drama and prose, but the syllabus of an English degree is now likely to include examples of the 'new media' and elements of creative writing. The 'literary' texts currently under examination in English departments could include graphic novels, blogs, advertisements, non-fictional essays and even public performances. On English degrees today, you may study Shakespeare alongside graffiti, compare Jane Austen's novels to *Sex and the City* or consider the similarities between the verse of the Romantic poets and the gangsta rap of Tupac Shakur. What all of these 'texts' have in common is that they are all in English, but there is not a sense of these being just about a literature of English*ness*. So how do we determine which texts in English should come under the rubric of literature?

The literary canon

Chris Baldick defines literature as 'a body of works that deserve to be preserved as part of the current reproduction of meanings within any given culture' (2001, 43). Traditionally, we think of literature as those laudable texts we *should* read and understand in order to become intellectually civilized members of our society. Granted, until the late twentieth century, studying literature was often a long-winded exercise in coming to terms with the poems, plays and works of fiction that elitist literary critics such as Matthew Arnold (1822–88) and F. R. Leavis (1895–1978) considered to be 'improving'. So how do 'literary' texts make it into the shortlist of those taught at the higher education level? This all comes down to the continuously evolving idea of what we call 'the literary canon'.

The idea of a literary canon is generally thought of as a list of those texts deemed worthy of inclusion on university syllabi. Historically, English literature has been about collecting together a body of literature that effectively demonstrates the values, mores, behaviours, cultural expectations, religious and political sensibilities of Englishness. It would be useful here to consider a brief history of the role of English literature as a tool of cultural indoctrination by the East India Company. Have you ever considered the logistics of how very few people from a tiny set of islands in the North Atlantic managed to gain so much power over the Indian subcontinent and its massive population? Lord Macaulay famously wrote in his *Minute on Indian Education* (1835), 'We must at present do our best to form a class who may be interpreters between us and the millions whom we govern – a class of persons Indian in blood and colour, but English in tastes, in opinions, in morals and in intellect' (Philips 1977, 1412). It was largely through a collection of 'literature of Englishness' – or what we now think of as 'canonical English literature' – that these ideas were dispersed amongst the Indian civil servants. Lord Macaulay and his colleagues in government were determined to 'civilize' these civil servants into an English way of thinking, so that they might impose rule on the population. Like all the best pyramid schemes, this enabled very few British leaders to rule over many millions of people, because they trained others to do the ruling for them. Just think – all this was accomplished with the help of literature!

Task – Make a quick list of the 30 most important texts you feel you should be studying in depth on an English literature degree. Are all of the writers originally from England? Is English their first language? Why might this be significant?

English literature and national identity

It did not take long for this idea of a literature of Englishness to become popular back in England. Peter Barry points out, 'There was, behind the teaching of early English, a distinctly Victorian mixture of class guilt about social inequalities, a genuine desire to improve things for everybody, a kind of missionary zeal to spread culture and enlightenment, and a self-interested desire to maintain social stability' (2002, 14). The inherent assumption here was that those who so hungrily received the teachings of English literature also bought into the idea that this literature represented a culture that somehow maintained a sense of moral, social, cultural and political superiority.

Clearly, this is no longer the case. Not only have the reasons for studying English literature changed, but the very idea of what it means to *be* English is continually evolving. What, then, does it mean to be English today? Surely the demise of the British Empire has left behind a legacy of English as a powerful lingua franca, but no longer can it be assumed that because one reads, writes, speaks and thinks in English that one *is* English. As a direct result of the aftermath of European colonization, English literature today is just as likely to include texts written in English by the postcolonial Nigerian writer Chinua Achebe and the Indian writer Arundhati Roy. Although the English language was initially introduced to the far reaches of the empire as a tool of colonial power, it has since served as a tool of rebellion – as a way of the former empire writing back to the colonial centre (see Ashcroft, Griffiths and Tiffin 1993 for a full discussion of this idea). Rather than something used to subjugate indigenous peoples, English has been reclaimed and wielded by many postcolonial writers as a tool of resistance – writers from all over the world can now claim variations of the English language as their own.

English as an academic discipline

If we briefly consider the path the study of English has taken to become a respected academic discipline, we will see that it has not always been this way. The closest thing to studying English at a university level for centuries was the study of classics – that is, ancient Greek and Latin literature. Of course many people read what we now consider to be 'exemplary' works of literature with an eye to improving their knowledge and cultural understanding, but the idea that such literature in English might be worthy of academic study did not receive any real support until English was first included as a subject of academic study at University College London in 1828. Even then, as Peter Barry points out, the course was largely based on 'the study of English language, with literature simply providing a rich source of linguistic examples' (2002, 14). It was at King's College London that English literature was first introduced as a university subject, in 1831. Barry (2002) and Eaglestone (2002) have produced comprehensive histories of the rise of English literature as a discipline, but suffice to say it was only taken seriously enough to be introduced as a degree subject at Oxford in 1884 and at Cambridge in 1911. Interestingly, although women were allowed to study English at university from around 1881, they were not allowed to actually take English *degrees* until 1920!

Career possibilities for English graduates

Today, English is one of the most popular humanities subjects studied at university level. Professor Maureen Moran suggests that by doing English, 'you develop the insight of an artist, the analytical precision of a scientist and the persuasiveness of a lawyer' (from the *Why Study English?* leaflet produced by the English Subject Centre, HEA). The skills you develop throughout an English degree can enable you to work in a surprising variety of jobs. Some of the graduates from our

English joint honours degrees at Solent University have gone on to work in: television research; copywriting and copyediting; writing erotica; advertising for the music industry; charity fundraising; publishing; teaching English as a foreign language; postgraduate study; primary and secondary school teaching; and developing educational resources for arts and heritage industries.

Task – Consider this: all of these are English graduates:

- Steven Fry (actor, writer, director, national treasure)

- Rosamund Pike (actress)

- Ian Hislop (editor of *Private Eye*)

- Mark Knopfler (guitarist and singer from Dire Straits)

- Charlotte Green (BBC TV journalist)

- Colin Greenwood (musician with Radiohead)

- Jemima Khan (UNICEF special representative)

- Tom Wilkinson (actor)

- Sir Ian Blair (former Metropolitan Police commissioner)

- Mark Ellingham (co-founder of the *Rough Guides*)

- Quentin Blake (author and illustrator of children's books)

You can see from this list that the possible career paths are hugely varied. Make a list of 20 other possible career paths you could imagine for graduates of English degrees.

Careers in teaching English

My time spent at university was the experience of a lifetime, academically and socially. The course itself was everything I had been looking for, a diverse and exciting timetable – my favourite unit was Storytelling – and the tutors provided me with the support I needed to succeed, with inspiring lectures and motivating enthusiasm. Because of my degree I now work as a learning support assistant in a college, helping individuals with learning disabilities experience education as I did, with a positive attitude and passionate support. I love my job and have Solent to thank for it.

(Chloe, graduate, BA (Hons) English and Screenwriting)

Many graduates fall in love with their subject, so the prospect of spending their working lives introducing others to the joys of English is an obvious career choice. In order to become a teacher within the state or independent school systems, you must do a one-year Postgraduate Certificate of Education (PGCE) course. Keep in mind that if you wish to teach primary school, you will be required to have passed your Maths and English GCSEs at a minimum grade of 'C' in order to be eligible to apply for the PGCE course. Additionally, you must have a minimum of two weeks' experience working in a school of the level you hope to teach. Competition is fierce, so I would recommend you aim for at least one month's experience if possible before even making the application. If you want to teach in the higher education sector, you'll need to do at least a master's degree in the relevant discipline, and most likely an MPhil (master of philosophy), leading to a PhD (doctor of philosophy) research degree in a relevant discipline. In rare circumstances, students can progress directly towards the PhD without the MPhil stage, but this varies between institutions. This can take anywhere from three to eight years. You'll also need to complete a one-year Post Graduate Certificate of Learning and Teaching in Higher Education (PGCLTHE) or the equivalent, in order to be able to teach in a university setting. Finally, if you want to teach in higher education, you will need at least four solid publications in academic, peer-reviewed journals or the equivalent. When I mentioned this long path to one of my first-year undergraduates years ago in response to his question, What would I need to do to earn the title, doctor of English? he paled, gulped and knuckled down to earn an excellent first-class degree. He is now enrolled on a master's course and well on the way to achieving his longed-for goal. It is essential that throughout your degree studies you manage to fit in some quality, solid work experience in addition to your studies. Those who finish with magnificent degrees but without work experience will find it much harder to break into the labour market than those students with solid degrees and a host of work experience. For now, though, let's focus on the various facets of an English degree.

Demystifying the characteristics of an English degree

One of the most useful aspects of an English degree is the focus on critical analysis. For students of English language, this will largely be in the form of *linguistic analyses* – that is, the close study of how language is used in various texts. By considering various linguistic aspects of English, such as the *phonology* (the sound systems of language), the *lexicon* (the choice of vocabulary used), the *morphology* (the structure of words), the *syntax* (the way words are used grammatically to form sentences), and the *semantics* (the meaning of language as opposed to its form), a linguistic analysis will uncover the significance of the language used in a text in order to understand more about the culture in which the text was produced. In order to produce a successful linguistic analysis, you must put on your close-up spectacles and uncover the fine details of the language used in a text.

Task – Consider this extract from Lewis Carroll's *Through the Looking Glass and What Alice Found There* **(1872):**

Twas brillig, and the slithy toves

Did gyre and gimble in the wabe:

All mimsy were the borogoves,

And the mome raths outgrabe.

Even though this is largely comprised of nonsense words, it evokes a very specific sense of environment. Why might this be? Do the morphology, semantics, syntax and phonology of these words perhaps play a more significant role than the – albeit nonstandard – actual lexicon?

For students of English literature as opposed to English language, the majority of assessments (whether essay, exam, seminar presentation or discussion) will be informed by *literary analyses*. Although there are necessarily some overlaps with linguistic analyses, the literary analysis tends to view the context in which a text is produced or studied in order to understand it more fully. English degree students today may draw from the disciplines of anthropology, psychology, philosophy, history or other cultural studies in order to find theoretical 'spectacles' through which to 'read' texts. What we must remember is that in contemporary English studies, there is no single right way to 'read' a text. Instead, as we hone our analytical tools, we are more and more able to assume responsibility for our textual readings – this does not mean that anything goes, but that there are many possible 'correct' readings of any given text. All of our analyses will be influenced by our own cultural/social/political/religious/economic positioning, as none of us can read a text as if we are a blank slate ready to be filled. We are all biased readers – and writers.

A literary analysis often begins with an *intrinsically* focused study of the words on the page. From this, we can begin to determine several things about the text: how it is packaged and framed, who is telling the story, if the narrator is reliable or unreliable, who holds the power in the story, and who the intended audience might be. From here, we can move outwards into an *extrinsically* focused study of various contextual elements of the text. If a linguistic analysis is largely about 'how' language is used in a text, a literary analysis tends to ask different questions: Who wrote it? Why? For whom was it written? Which texts were published in the same genre during the same period of time? Was this written by a man or a woman? Why might this be significant? What a literary analysis *is not* is a biographical overview of the author's life and times. It *is* a focused reading of a text using various theoretical approaches as 'spectacles' through which to consider various aspects of the writing. It is important to come to terms with the difference between these two kinds of analyses before submitting your first marked assessment for your degree. Be clear you understand exactly what your tutor expects from you and you'll be on the road to success.

What to Do before Your Degree

> Be sure to get all of the books on the reading list well in advance, and try to get through them all over the summer before the first term begins. I thought it would be fine to read as I went along, but it was almost impossible to keep up with the huge reading lists! I learned quickly, and for the second term, I made sure I was ready by reading all of the books over the Christmas holidays.
>
> (Ray, BA (Hons) English and Film)

> Don't be afraid to e-mail or call the course leader for advice, even before the course starts. They are very happy to help you out and they usually don't bite.
>
> (Harriet, BA (Hons) English and Magazine Journalism)

> Remember, you are not expected to know everything about degree-level studies before you arrive – you're here to learn this stuff!
>
> (Jane, BA (Hons) English and Writing Contemporary Fiction)

By the end of this section, you should have some idea of:

- how current students prepared for their English literature degree
- how they would have prepared in hindsight
- the advice lecturers give about preparing for an English literature degree

- why it is a good idea to get the reading lists in advance

- some of the challenges of making the transition from studying at school or college to degree level

- how mature students can signal their need for aid in advance of the course

- how students with special needs *must* signal their need for aid in advance of the course

- how to balance your outside responsibilities with the demands of the course

What makes a good student of English?

I thoroughly enjoyed studying English and Magazine Journalism at Solent. As a Slovakian student, this gave me an opportunity to significantly improve my language and writing skills, enhance my creativity, and develop my ability to work independently. Experience gave me the confidence to tackle the world of publishing and freelance journalism. I discovered you don't have to be English to enjoy studying English!

(Domi, graduate, BA (Hons) English and Magazine Journalism)

It's a good idea to consider what makes a good English student long before you actually begin your degree studies. As with everything in life, the more you put into your degree, the more you will get out of it. Over your three (or four years if you are taking a study abroad year) years of study, you will encounter many different, wonderful works of fiction, poetry and drama. You will study literature, language, culture and history in considerable depth.

You will develop your research, writing, analytical and communication skills. You will learn to think in new and imaginative ways. By the end of it, you will have developed your knowledge and understanding, your intellectual and academic abilities, and your practical and creative skills in the discipline of English, to become an intelligent, motivated and imaginative potential employee. This will of course require a lot of input from you.

Some of the most important things we'll ask of you include:

A passion for reading. If you don't enjoy literature and language, frankly, you shouldn't be studying it! We expect you to read regularly for pleasure as well as for your studies. Remember Professor Melrose's suggestion that 'better readers make better thinkers make better writers'.

Commitment. We will ask you to do a lot of reading, and we do not expect you to come to classes unprepared. You will do all the reading that is set, and more!

Regular attendance. You must attend all timetabled classes, and if you are unable to attend, you will inform the relevant tutor in advance. You will catch up on any classes you miss by talking with classmates or tutors, and catch up on any relevant reading. Unexplained absences should always be followed up by the course team.

Participation. Much of the teaching on English degrees takes the form of seminars. These are group discussions, and they work best when everyone in the room makes verbal contributions throughout.

Willingness to debate. You must thoroughly prepare and have confidence in your own thoughts and opinions, whilst showing respect for those of other class members. Productive debate is about sharing, clarifying, reflecting upon and questioning one another's ideas in an informed manner; it is very different from aggressive or petulant squabbling. Remember, too, that your tutors are there to engage in debate – be willing to challenge them if you disagree.

Self-motivation and discipline. The vast majority of your studies take place in your own time, and this means you will have to manage your time effectively. Of course you will want to enjoy the social aspects of university life, and you may need to support yourself with part-time work. Neither of these, however, should interfere with your studies, and if you find they are, you should speak to the course team for guidance.

Initiative. The very best English students will not wait to be told to do something: they will identify subjects they wish to research, or skills they wish to develop, and set about it. The course team are always more than happy to provide guidance on self-directed study.

Creativity. English is above all a creative subject, and those who are willing to think 'outside the box' and to engage with unfamiliar ideas always do well. Don't be afraid of developing your own voice, writing style or intellectual approach – this is the very lifeblood of the subject.

Preparing for the adventure ahead. There are ways to prepare yourself for the rigours of degree-level study in addition to ploughing through the reading lists. If you don't already do so, it is a good idea to start reading a broadsheet newspaper to keep up with what is happening in the world.

Task – Clip articles regarding interesting current events in literature, language or English in higher education from the weekend papers. Just one per week will do the trick. You will soon begin to see a pattern in how literary issues are represented in the media, which will be fabulous preparation for your university-level English studies. Keep these in a folder so you can refer to them during seminar discussions.

Also, it would be useful to remind yourself of some of the major historical events over the past few hundred years – although English degrees are clearly not history degrees, a working understanding of broad historical and political developments will only enhance your literary studies and potentially improve your written responses to the texts you'll be studying.

Another easily overlooked skill is touch-typing. It is ironic that even in our current rapidly evolving academic environment, we still depend on technology that is more than a hundred years old – the QWERTY keyboard. (If you wonder where this odd name comes from, have a look at your English computer keyboard and it will be obvious.) Would you believe this was originally created to slow typists down, as the romantic old mechanical typewriters couldn't cope with high speeds? Contemporary keyboards can cope with rapid-fire speeds, and having this handy skill will make your life much easier when you're frantically trying to get your essays done on time.

Task – Find a free 'Teach Yourself to Touch-Type' programme online and start on the road to freedom! Challenge yourself to learn all of the letters without looking within a month, and then the numbers within another month. The punctuation is different on different keyboards, so you'll need to assess these individually.

Do I need any special equipment?

I was so relieved to find out that it would be no problem to look for my course books in charity shops. Before uni started, I dreaded being skint and living on a tight budget, but my flatmates and I all mucked in together and found great deals on food and study materials, and we had a sort of competition to find the best second-hand books!

(Joe, BA (Hons) English and Film)

Parents often ask me what sort of equipment their son or daughter will need in order to succeed on an English degree. My response? Something to write with and something to write on. English is one of the more affordable degrees, as no real specialist equipment is required. One of my students was delighted to purchase all of her second-year primary texts for under £20 by scouring second-hand book shops. You should be able to check out all of the books you'll need from the university library, or you may choose to purchase your own new or second-hand copies. Your tutors will indicate if you must have a particular edition of a text. Many students prefer accessing their books electronically via an e-reader, which is an affordable and convenient option. Do keep in mind, though, that electronic devices are not usually allowed in open-book exams, so you may eventually need to obtain print copies of certain texts. All universities have IT centres with access to computers, printers, scanning equipment, etc., and these often have extended opening hours. Although it is certainly not required, most students find it convenient to have their own computer whenever possible, as demand is high and the wait for a slot may be long during peak times such as before important deadlines. If you live in student halls, you may well be networked into the university Internet system, but it is important to check first to avoid disappointment.

From A-level to degree

Many students find the transition from school or college to degree-level studies challenging, as the learning cultures tend to be quite different. One of the biggest surprises to many first-year English students is that they are not being directed to a 'correct' reading of a text. Instead, they are introduced to a variety of theoretical perspectives, any of which could potentially offer the 'spectacles' through which to interpret various viewpoints and possible readings. At university, students are expected to engage with at least three hours of outside reading/study for every hour they spend in class. Thus, for a typical 14-hour weekly contact time with your tutors through lectures, seminars and workshops, you are expected to spend at least another 42 hours reading and studying. More than 50 hours studying per week doesn't leave much time for a job, if you want to succeed academically. Of course, much of your reading can be done in places other than the library – in bed, in the bath or even in the park. Put this way, spending so many hours per week doing something you love (i.e., reading and writing about reading) is a rather appealing way of spending three years! Going away to university is meant to be fun as well as academically challenging, but for some mature students who are juggling young families and outside responsibilities with their longed-for university studies, it is essential to organize a support network long before you even begin the course.

Mature students and degree studies

Life can be challenging when you struggle with learning difficulties and mobility issues, which made embarking on an academic pathway at 52 an altogether daunting prospect for me.

I needn't have worried. Solent has an amazing support network that was in place from the very early days helping me to put learning strategies in place. The course itself was fabulously structured so there was never a dull moment, each term presenting me with new challenges that always led to new milestones to celebrate. There are plenty of visiting professionals to help you plan how you will apply your new skills to your career plan.

Since graduating, I have returned to my business, which has since had a major facelift. I am now teaching art to adults, and putting together a programme which embraces bespoke skills and methodology of applied art. I am also writing course notes, technical guides and instruction notes in addition to long-term projects in creative writing. Gaining my degree has given me an indelible confidence in pushing myself forward *knowing* my skills, not simply assuming I have them because I had worked in the industry for so long. I didn't. I had complacency. Now I have a degree. Priceless.

(Katey, graduate, BA (Hons) English and Screenwriting)

For mature students, it can be helpful to ask your course leader to put you into contact with other mature students on the course well before the course begins. Just knowing you are not the only older student on the course can boost your confidence. If you are a carer or have disabilities that might impact your learning, it is important you communicate your concerns with your tutor before the course begins. Extra student support is available, but demand tends to be high so you must try to put your support package in place long before you arrive. Most universities provide ample online materials to support in-class learning, and most now provide the option of submitting assessments online wherever possible.

In an ideal world, every student will have a quiet, peaceful corner to study where they are unlikely to be disturbed. For those students juggling young families, this doesn't have to be an impossibility. You may find that your only realistic study time is either when the little ones are napping or after they have gone to bed in the evening, when you'd rather slurp a glass of wine and collapse into a comfortable chair. Keeping your goal of earning that degree in mind can really help you stay focused. Some of the most significant works of English literature throughout history were created by busy women with large families; they stole time at their kitchen tables to create their works of genius, one paragraph at a time. Try to find just a small space somewhere where you can leave piles of books and papers undisturbed, and where you can escape to write, read and think. Reminding your nearest and dearest that with a degree, you're more likely to secure a good job to help the family will doubtless smooth any potential tensions that may arise from your understandably divided attentions.

Task – Make a list of 10 ways in which having a good university degree is going to improve your life and the lives of your closest family members. Refer to this when the going gets rough!

Many students find it helpful to access unabridged audiobook versions of the primary readings, so they can listen as they read. What is absolutely not recommended, however, is falling into the trap of thinking you needn't read *Middlemarch* because you've seen the TV miniseries. Film adaptations are not novels and there really is no substitute for engaging with the primary text itself – so get reading.

Making the Most of Your Learning

The shift from college, where things are quite structured and you are told what to do and where/when/how to do it, to university, where you are expected to be a fully functioning adult, can be quite a shock. Not only is it the first time many of us are having to shop, cook, clean and do laundry for ourselves, but it is often the first time in our lives when no one is making us get up and perform! At first it is a relief to have some independence, but it can be tough to keep up the motivation to get to class on time and get all of your work done on time, especially if you've been out partying with your mates the night before.

My advice is not to take on an outside job until you really get to grips with how things work at university, or the job will begin to take over your time and your studies will really suffer. Sometimes we have to work to survive, but if you can give yourself even one term before you start a job, you'll give yourself a good chance of developing some good study habits.

(David, BA (Hons) English and Advertising)

By the end of this section, you should have some idea of:

- the differences between lectures, seminars and tutorials

- how to make the most of each of these learning environments

- how to take good notes and use the VLE effectively

- your role as an independent learner

University teaching environments

The majority of the teaching in higher education is done through lectures, seminars and tutorials. It might seem obvious, but you do need to show up and participate in these sessions if you hope to succeed in your assessments. Please don't fall into the trap of feeling you can learn everything you need to know by getting notes from your mates and reading widely. You are paying hugely for the privilege of studying at university, and it is only common sense to avail yourself of all the learning opportunities on offer. Joe Sarnowski argues that the real value of a higher education is that it 'provides students with the *opportunity* to grow intellectually, to learn how to learn, to discover how to work under deadlines and to solve problems'. He goes on to suggest that the final degree 'is not the product that students purchase with tuition: the process is the product' (2014).

If students choose not to engage with the learning opportunities available to them during their time as an undergraduate, they will not be developing those skills future employers are looking for. Arguably, such students should necessarily include what Sarnowski describes as 'people who have engaged with a rigorous, demanding process and have completed their work conscientiously'. The days of just showing up for the exams after spending three years drinking champagne and punting on the river are long gone (if they ever existed – *Brideshead Revisited* has a lot to answer for). Each university has its own attendance policy, but if you do not show up for a period of time with no communication to your course leader, you are likely to be withdrawn from the course – but you are still financially responsible for the student loan you took out for the year's fees! My advice is to fully commit to the course or it really won't be worth your while.

You should be given a unit handbook (or the verbal equivalent) which outlines the teaching schedule, the assessments, the learning outcomes and an indicative reading list. There will be several different methods of teaching on your degree course.

The lecture

Lectures include the whole student group for a unit (this can be anywhere from around twenty to around five hundred students) and usually last just under an hour. The lecture is where the main ideas are presented and technical terms introduced and unpacked. For these to make sense, you must do the required reading beforehand. During lectures, it is usual for the tutor to speak in a structured, sometimes formal way, and for students to listen and take careful notes. The lecturer may pause occasionally to take questions, but these are usually kept for the end of the session.

If the tutor uses technical terms you don't understand, do write them down so you can ask for clarification later. The tutor may use PowerPoint, smart boards or other educational technologies, or they may simply speak to the group. If, due to a special learning need, you would find it helpful for tutors to use a particular colour/size/font for their presentations or handouts, do let them know ahead of time. Learning materials, including lecture slides if they are used, notes and readings, should be available weekly on the virtual learning environment (VLE; see below). It is important to arrive on time (or even a few minutes early) for lectures, as the lecturer will not have time to go back over any material you may have missed if you come in late to the session – habitual lateness is downright rude.

Taking useful notes

However good the online resources to support your course, there is no substitute for carefully listening to the lectures and taking good notes in a legible format. For some students, pen and paper will suffice, but for others, a laptop or tablet computer with a keyboard docking station is more appropriate. If you would like to digitally sound record any lectures, *you must ask the tutor's permission in advance* – they may even make a podcast of the lecture available if you give them ample advance notice to arrange the recording equipment. Some students much prefer to record lectures, and simply listen during the session, only writing down their notes when they revisit the recorded lecture later. Many tutors will supply either a handout or a set of notes on the VLE, which you can print out and bring to the lecture to aid your note taking. There are many good note-taking techniques, but the two most popular methods are the *outline* method and the *mind map* method.

The *outline* method can be successful if you are listening to a lecture by a tutor with a very structured, logical flow to the discussion. Tutors who clearly state the aims and objectives of each session beforehand (perhaps writing these down or showing them on a screen) and who clearly mention the main trajectory the lecture will take enable students to take traditional notes with topic headlines and bullet-pointed bits of information underneath these headings. Outlined notes are not in full sentences, but take the most important bits from the lecture and list them in a logical format. For linear, logical thinkers this is a very good method of recording information taken from lectures, but if either the student or the tutor tend to go off on tangents, the mind map method may be more appropriate.

The *mind map* begins with a single sheet of paper. Put the title of the lecture in the middle of the page and circle it. Then draw spokes out from this centre with each of the various aspects of the topic you come across during the session. Put smaller spokes out from these with the details you'd like to remember and the important points the tutor makes about each.

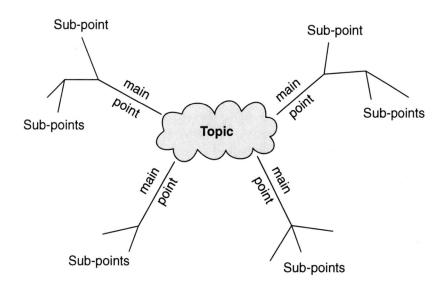

Don't feel you must write down everything the tutor says – this would be an exercise in futility – but do write down those points and ideas that jump out at you as significant. If you are not able to get down all of the information, do ask the tutor to clarify the points either after the lecture or in the seminar session. You may find it helpful to use different colours for different points, thus keeping your mind map more visually organized.

Task – Create a mind map of one of your favourite books. Start with the main characters, move out to the main themes, then start filling in specific examples. Try this with several different books and you'll soon get the hang of it.

The seminar

Seminars generally last from one to two hours and are much smaller and more relaxed affairs than lectures, usually with no more than 24 students in each seminar group, but this varies widely between institutions. This is your opportunity to discuss in depth the concepts introduced during the lecture, and to get answers for any questions you may have about the subject. The room will be set up to enable discussion between students and tutor, so tables or desks will probably be arranged in a horseshoe or semicircle shape rather than in rows facing the front. As ever, it is essential you do all of the required reading in advance. You must expect to be called on to explain a passage of text or to use a particular theoretical approach to read a selection of verse, and it can be exceedingly embarrassing if you have not done any preparations. It is a good idea to exchange mobile numbers and e-mail addresses with several members of your seminar group, as you may well want to meet up to study or discuss the texts in between formally scheduled sessions. Quite often, seminars are student led, with the tutor there to ensure the discussion stays on track. If you are naturally shy, seminars can provide a safe place to practice speaking in front of others to gain confidence in your own ideas. Many institutions build collaborative learning and group work into their seminar design – this can be either formative (i.e., an essential component of the learning process, but not marked in such a way that it contributes to your final degree classification) or summative (i.e., actually contributing to your final degree classification).

The tutorial

Tutorials are the one-to-one sessions you have with your tutor, which can be either weekly or can be scheduled as and when you feel the need. During tutorials, you can communicate your ideas and your concerns directly to your tutor, knowing they are giving you their full attention. Generally tutorials are for academic discussions, but they can also be the first port of call if you are experiencing personal difficulties with your studies, as your tutors can guide you towards whatever appropriate support services the university has to offer. Some students feel awkward at first when meeting individually with their tutors, but it gets easier and this should be a very productive part of your learning process. Your tutor will draw answers out of you during tutorials, and will probably ask you to defend your position on various literary issues.

To make the most of the tutorial environment, be sure to write down in advance any questions or concerns you have so they don't slip your mind.

If there are books you need but have not been able to access, do ask your tutor, who may be able to order copies for the university library.

The virtual learning environment

The virtual learning environment (or VLE) is one of the most useful tools at your disposal as an undergraduate student. Lecture notes, lecture slides, links to essential readings, glossaries, timetables, recommended readings and even internship possibilities will be available through this electronic resource. Some units may include a class discussion forum or blog as part of the learning process, and this can be found on the VLE. It is important to remember to enrol yourself on each of your scheduled units, so you'll have full access to all the VLE has on offer. This will also ensure you receive group e-mail messages about any course changes or notices.

One of the biggest challenges for first-year students is understanding that learning effectively becomes *your* responsibility when you reach university. Your tutors make all of the information available to you, but they will not have the time to introduce you to every concept and idea you need to learn to succeed on the course. They are there as subject specialists to guide you through your studies and point you towards essential readings, but they cannot do the reading and thinking for you – that is your job. You will be expected to spend at least two or three hours in the library reading for each hour spent in lectures/seminars. Many students find developing the skills to conduct independent research daunting. When you are searching for appropriate sources for information to support your learning, there are a few things that will make the process more straightforward. When you are taking notes from texts, it can be challenging working out what is important enough to write down and what should be left out. There's no right or wrong way to take notes from your sources, but if you have trouble, it may be worth trying the **SQRRR** technique:

- **Scan:** A quick flick through, get an overall impression.
- **Questions:** Who? What? Where? Why? When? How?
- **Read:** Read the text carefully.
- **Remember:** Jot down the main points without looking at the text.
- **Review:** Read the passage again, taking notes.

Remember, you should *always keep records*. Write down author name, book or journal title, page numbers and any other information you'll need to re-access or correctly cite your information. This is one of the major changes between learning in tertiary and in higher education: you must become far more responsible and independent and will not be able to rely on your tutor to remember the publication details of each and every quote.

Task – Make a short bibliography of twenty or so of the books you have on hand. Be sure to put this into the correct format for your own university's English department. It is very helpful to get into the habit of doing this correctly even before the assessments begin.

Deadlines and extensions for assessments

You will be told all deadlines for assessments at the beginning of each term (and these are available on the VLE and in the unit handbooks) but *you will probably not be reminded about these*, as it is assumed that as adult, independent learners, you take the responsibility for your own time management regarding deadlines. If you miss deadlines, you lose marks or may well earn a mark of zero for the assessment, so do get in the habit early on of turning in your best work on time.

Please don't take it for granted that you will be granted extensions for late work. Every institution has its own policies regarding late work – ours allows students to submit work up to 10 working days late, at a penalty of losing one grade mark. Others may allow summer resits, but these are usually capped at the lowest passing mark, so the risk to your potential degree success is enormous. Check carefully to ensure you understand the rules around assessment submission.

How to Pass Your First Assignments and Exams

Even though my tutors kept saying to follow the brief and keep to the point of a task, I honestly thought they were just trying to get me to dumb down my writing style, which is naturally creative and energetic. I was shocked when my first essay came back with a terrible mark. I thought it was so good – but I guess I didn't pay attention to what they were asking for. I learned my lesson – next time, I'm booking tutorials with my lecturers and finding out exactly what they are looking for!

(Jonathan, BA (Hons) English and Public Relations)

By the end of this section, you should have some idea of:

- how to understand course learning outcomes

- first-year assessments and grading bands

- how to use marking criteria to improve and understand your own work

- how to research/write a successful essay

- how to heighten your understanding of how exam questions are written from learning outcomes

- how to revise and prepare for assessments and exams

Many first-year students find the first assessment extremely difficult. There is likely to be much less guidance on how a particular topic should be addressed than is provided in school- or college-level study. The tendency is to present the student with choices they can investigate themselves, with a focus on independent learning. This chapter aims to introduce you to the idea of learning outcomes, grade bands and the sort of marking criteria your tutors are likely to use when marking your work. Although you might not be able to work out which specific questions are likely to feature in an exam or timed assessment, a clear understanding of the unit learning outcomes will give you a good idea of the sorts of areas you will be expected to master throughout the unit. It is important to remember that at university level, doing English is not about being able to memorize a long list of dates and authors. Instead, the focus of exam questions is likely to be testing your 'big picture' understanding of the ideas and texts discussed, as well as the quality and persuasiveness of your argument/discussion. If your answers evidence your understanding of how a specific text fits into the bigger picture of historical literary production, it will impress the examiner more than the ability to reel off a string of accurate dates.

Course learning outcomes

Every unit you take has a list of *course learning outcomes*, and these should be available to you on the VLE as well as in each individual unit handbook. These are broken down into several categories: Knowledge and Understanding (**K**), Cognitive Skills (**C**), Practical and Professional Skills (**P**) and Transferable and Key Skills (**T**). Typically, **K** outcomes include the sorts of subject-specific ideas and concepts you will clearly understand upon successful completion of the unit.

Here are two examples of the sorts of **K** skills I would expect students to understand upon completion of the first-year Adapting the Novel unit:

> **K1:** Identify, explain and discuss key concepts studied on the unit, including: realism, modernism, postmodernism, the rise of the novel, canon, plot, genre, characterization, structure, narrative techniques and intertextuality.

> **K2:** Identify the major themes/issues raised by these novels and how their adaptations reflect social change.

These give you clear guidance to the concepts and ideas you'll need to know and understand in order to succeed in your assessments. If you find you can discuss these ideas with ease during seminars and tutorials, you can be confident that you are well on the way to being prepared for the assessments.

The **C** skills tend to focus on how your growing understanding of technical concepts and theoretical stances can be useful across the range of units on your degree course. Typical **C** skills might be as follows:

> **C1:** Apply concepts, theories and methods studied to examine and interpret possible meanings of written and filmic examples and their effects.

> **C2:** Apply an understanding of critical traditions and terminology to a scholarly study of novels and film/television adaptations of these novels.

These skills demonstrate that you have not only learned and understood some of the major ideas on the unit, but that you can apply them practically.

The **P** skills include the sorts of skills that form an integral part of the skillset English literature students must have to be able to cope with the rigours of the course. Typical **P** skills might read as follows:

> **P1:** Reliably source data using basic research skills and reference sources using correct academic protocols.

> **P2:** Apply the skills of close textual analysis to interpret canonical works of fiction and film.

During the first year of your degree, you will be developing and honing your skills of academic writing, research and close textual analysis. You will also begin to improve the skills which will ensure you are highly employable upon successful completion of your degree course – your transferable and key skills. Typical **T** skills might include:

T1: Work independently and communicate relevant information and ideas in coherent written form.

T2: Communicate knowledge, understanding and evaluative skills by producing lucid, evidenced written accounts and arguments using proper academic citations.

Style and formatting for assessments

One of the most frustrating areas for many first-year students is referencing and coming to terms with the written style and format your assessments are meant to take. It is essential that you clarify with each of your tutors exactly the style in which they prefer essays to be written. Some tutors insist on double spacing, some on certain fonts or font sizes. Find out exactly which referencing system they prefer and realize that different tutors have different requirements. This can be annoying, but it is excellent training for the professional working world, in which you will doubtless be required to follow a different house style for different writing tasks. You may be asked to use Harvard (parenthetical) referencing, or you may be asked to use endnotes or footnotes. It is important to obtain the department's style sheet and learn their preferred system of referencing during your first term.

Grade marking

Many universities use the A–F grade banding system, whilst others use the numerical system, in which work can earn a mark from 0–100 per cent, with 40 per cent being the lowest passing mark and 55 per cent the average. It can be a shock for first-year students used to earning marks well in the 80 per cent range when they arrive at university and proudly turn in their first essay, only to gasp in horror at their first (very respectable) mark of 62 per cent. This equates to a B grade in most institutions. You should check each individual assignment for specific marking criteria, but your work will generally be assessed on the following:

- focus on the topic
- sophistication of ideas
- coherence of discussion

• clarity of expression

• technical accuracy (i.e., spelling/grammar)

• evidence of secondary research

Your work will be given a percentage mark based on these criteria; the pass mark is 40 per cent, and a mark below this means you have failed to meet the assessment criteria. Below is the grade banding currently used at Solent University:

Class	Grade point on scale	Solent grade	Numerical equivalent
First	Excellent 1st	**A1**	100
	High 1st	**A2**	92
	Mid 1st	**A3**	83
	Low 1st	**A4**	72
Upper second	High 2.1	**B1**	68
	Mid 2.1	**B2**	65
	Low 2.1	**B3**	62
Lower second	High 2.2	**C1**	58
	Mid 2.2	**C2**	55
	Low 2.2	**C3**	52
Third	High 3rd	**D1**	48
	Mid 3rd	**D2**	45
	Low 3rd	**D3**	42
Fail	Marginal fail	**F1**	38
	Fail	**F2**	30
	Mid fail	**F3**	20
	Low fail	**F4**	15
Submitted	Submitted	**S**	1
Non-submission	Non-submission	**N**	0

Here's a guide to what these grades mean:

% Grade	Characteristics of % Grade Band
0%	Penalty grade for academic malpractice.
1–9%	Of no relevance whatsoever to the objectives of the module assessment.
10–19%	Very little of any relevance or substance. Lacking in application or quality.
20–34%	An attempt has been made to address the relevant issues. However, it is still mainly of little relevance or is scanty and backed up with little or no evidence. The style may be inappropriate, with serious errors of grammar, spelling and structure. Displays some intellectual or practical application.
35–39%	Some relevant issues are addressed. However, the answer is largely descriptive or anecdotal, or is backed up with little evidence. The style may be inappropriate, with serious errors of grammar, spelling and structure. Inability to handle knowledge; limitations in practical skills.
40–49% (third class / 3rd)	The main issues have been addressed, but there may be some omissions. There is little theoretical content. The style may be inappropriate, with errors of grammar, spelling and structure. Limited in interpretative use of knowledge or in some practical skills.
50–59% (lower second class / 2:2)	A competent answer, which addresses the main issues satisfactorily, but which may contain minor omissions or errors. Theoretical issues are addressed, but may be somewhat superficial. There is a degree of appreciation of the material, but this may show limited evidence of critical ability. The style is largely good. Good grasp of knowledge and practice with some limitations.
60–69% (upper second class / 2:1)	All main issues addressed with clarity. There is evidence of wide reading. The work is well organized with relevant arguments cogently developed and supported by appropriate evidence. There is evidence of considerable critical and analytical ability, with clear insights and competent evaluation of material. It is well presented and structured. The grammar and style are good. Good capacity to interpret and use material flexibly, no practical inadequacies. At the higher margin work will not contain any errors or omissions.
70–79% (first class / 1st)	Highly critical and analytical, well presented and structured, with a comprehensive and insightful exposition of relevant theory and research. Demonstrates creative flair or excellent skill in performance linked with strong interpretative understanding.
80–89% (first class / 1st)	As 70–79%, but makes innovative or original links with related theory and/or research. May be of publishable quality. Creative flair combined with strong interpretative understanding.
90–100% (first class / 1st)	As 80–89% but highly original or innovative, or creates an entirely new synthesis of ideas. Of publishable quality. Creative flair combined with profound interpretative understanding.

Essays

During your first year, you are likely to come across a variety of assessment types, but the most common will be the essay. This is a formal, academic, literary analysis of a particular topic, and will follow a very specific style. The best book I've come across to take you through the finer aspects of undergraduate essay writing is Chris Mounsey's *One Step Ahead: Essays and Dissertations* (2002). The important thing to remember is that a successful essay does not need to tell the marker everything there is to know about a subject. Rather, an essay is a focused, targeted discussion of one aspect of a topic that demonstrates to the marker that you can not only introduce an argument, but that you can also support your points with scholarly secondary sources which further the discussion. You must come to a conclusion, but this need not be the only possible conclusion in the world – it is simply the logical conclusion you've reached after going through the process of considering various points of view.

Academic essays need to do a few things: 1) *they need to answer the question* – first, define the question's parameters, then identify the key debates it references, then define the key critical terms it uses; 2) *they need to present a logical, cogent, well-argued response to the question* – first, they must show an awareness of the critical debates you have been invited to engage with on your unit, then they must present an argument in response to those debates; 3) *they need to demonstrate the validity of your argument with proof* – this means the arguments must be supported with critical evidence via quotes from relevant, academically sound critical secondary sources, as well as referencing examples from the primary texts. All of these enable you to successfully argue a case.

Many undergraduates groan at the necessity to use secondary critical material to underpin their work – they feel that their opinions are all that really matters! Of course they matter – but only insofar as they can be supported by the academically recognized work of those scholars who have already made their mark on academia.

You should give yourself as much time as possible to research, plan and write an essay. It is not a good idea to wait until the night before the deadline! You generally choose to respond to one from a list of several questions. It is essential you always stick to the brief. By carefully reading the assessment brief, you will be able to determine a few important things:

1. What choices is it offering?
2. Exactly what it is asking you to do?
3. Exactly what it is asking you to focus on?
4. Is there more than one part to the question?

You may already know lots about the subject in question, but you do need to determine the weaker areas of your knowledge/understanding to help you focus your research. Look over your lecture/seminar notes, but remember these are simply a starting point for your research – you cannot simply vomit these out on paper and expect them to contribute to a fully formed essay!

Researching for an essay

Now for the exciting bit – the research itself. Get thyself to your university library, look up the topic on the library search system, and get to the appropriate aisle. Don't simply limit yourself to books on the exact subject of your enquiry; spend quality time perusing the shelves on either side for alternate texts that may well be helpful for your project. Consider books, academic journals, newspapers, archived interviews, e-books and e-journals, and of course your helpful university librarian. The most important thing to remember is to keep constant, accurate records of the origins of each quote. You'll need to know the author, title, date of publication, publishing house, city and *page number*. Your research will begin to reveal information trails – bibliographies and footnotes are a wealth of information about alternate paths you could consider following towards your goal of a well-researched essay.

A word of warning – be very careful about using Internet sources, unless they come from a reliable, academic online journal (Literature Online, JSTOR and Academic OneFile are the most commonly used online academic resources used by English students). Avoid using any old website you've found on a Google search, as anyone could have written it. Avoid *Wikipedia* as it is rarely accurate. Finally, be sure you understand the seriousness of plagiarizing – it will result in your being kicked out of university. Plagiarizing is using the words or ideas of anyone else without giving them full credit for their words. It is easily avoided by maintaining excruciatingly careful records of where you found your quoted material.

Task – Choose a random topic and come up with a rough research question. Make a list of five possible approaches you might take to this question. Get yourself to a library (not online!) and find 10 possible books or journal articles that may have useful, relevant information that could help you contend with this topic. Think outside the box! Your ideas on the topic will naturally begin to change as your research reveals more and more exciting possibilities.

How to structure an essay

Now for the essay itself. Essays have four parts: 1) introduction, 2) main body, 3) conclusion, and 4) bibliography.

The introduction should be clear and grab the reader's attention. It must introduce which question you will be responding to, the primary texts you'll be considering, and an overview of the sorts of secondary theories you will be considering to support your argument.

The main body of the essay contains your main arguments as well as the supporting material to underpin these. Your job is to convince the reader of the truth of your argument, so you must be logical, authoritative and persuasive. It is best to plan your essay before you begin writing. Consider what each paragraph will accomplish – they should each revolve around a central point, highlighted in the first ('topic') sentence. Then provide your 'take' on this point, supported by evidence and examples. Finally, conclude each paragraph with a logical flow into the next, to maintain a sense of logical flow. Try not to waffle or overly pad out your work. Get to the point and ensure each point is underpinned by strong analysis. Stick to the topic – this is not just a chance to list facts and dates, but demands a clear and sophisticated analytical approach to the discussion.

The conclusion is an overview of the main points you have made in the essay, and brings it to a logical end. You do not use quotes in a conclusion, nor do you introduce new points or new topics of discussion. By the time you reach this stage in your writing, you may well be tired and fed up, but stick with it – the conclusion is one of the most important parts of your essay!

Remember, you must include a full bibliography of all of the texts (primary and secondary) you have used within the essay. Check your department style sheet to determine their preferred method of referencing. Be sure to proofread carefully. Errors in spelling, punctuation and grammar lose marks.

Task – Now go through your research from the previous task and try to identify three or four main areas about a particular topic that really interest you. Try to hone these down into three or four main points for discussion. How could you logically link these together to form the skeletal framework for a basic essay?

Other assessments

Essays are not the only method of assessing a first-year student's progress. Other typical assessments include portfolios, individual or group presentations and exams. The most important thing to keep in mind is that in order to pass, you must follow the brief, and be able to demonstrate (if asked) how your work provides evidence of your successful achievement of the learning outcomes of the unit. These can be found in the unit handbook. For example, if one of the outcomes is 'C1: Apply concepts, theories and methods studied to examine and interpret possible meanings of written and filmic examples and their affects', clearly you must understand the ideas you have studied on the unit and show that you can use these to analyse various texts. If the outcome is '**P1**: Reliably source data using basic research skills and reference sources using correct academic protocols', you will need to demonstrate how you use secondary critical quotes to correctly support your arguments.

Choosing Options and Their Implications

> I was lucky enough to get two fabulous options for my English degree – the chance to study Beginning Mandarin Chinese, and to engage in work-based learning. These weren't obviously related to my degree subject, but they were so useful and really did help me after graduation to find a decent job, as none of the other applicants knew another language! The work-based learning gave me the chance to get some valuable work experience in a literary field, as I managed to snag an internship at a publishing house.
>
> (Alice, BA (Hons) English and Advertising)

By the end of this section, you should have some idea of:

- understanding the option choices available to you on your degree

- your motivation for studying this degree

- your foreign language options

- some of your employability options

- the requirements for postgraduate study

- which assessment strategies would best suit your chances of success

This section explains the implications of students' module choices in the light of future employment opportunities and further study. Most English degrees will include an element of optionality – that is, you'll be able to choose from a selection of possible optional units in addition to the core units you must take to fulfil the requirements of the degree. Some universities enable students to take a purely literature-based pathway, some a purely language-based pathway, and some a creative writing–based pathway that includes elements of both literature and language, as we discussed earlier in this chapter.

In order to make an informed decision about which optional units will best suit your preferences, it is important to examine your personal motivation for studying for an English degree in the first place. Has your A-level English teacher ignited within you a passion for seventeenth-century poetry which won't be satisfied until you study literature at an intense level at university? If your dream is to become a novelist or a published poet, units on creative writing should figure into your choices. An English degree may be the obvious path towards future employment – perhaps you dream of being a secondary English teacher, in which case it is crucial you study Shakespeare's works on your degree. In our current competitive climate, it may be useful to have studied units on English language, as this may well enable you to teach on a greater variety of A-level English modules. If your dream is to work in the publishing industry, you may find a unit on the literary industry useful.

Besides choosing an option that appeals to you academically, it is also wise to find out how each option will be assessed. It is always sensible to choose optional units which will suit your individual strengths, and those in which you feel you are the most likely to achieve higher marks. For example, if you tend to find exam situations exceedingly stressful, choosing an optional unit that is assessed only by exam is not advisable. If you find group assessments challenging, avoid those units with a heavy weighting towards group marks.

Some universities offer optional units clearly focused on employability skills, such as CV building and interview techniques, community volunteering or foreign-language study, which may be helpful to your future career in today's increasingly global marketplace. Don't forget that most universities will also have the option of taking a term or a year abroad in another country as a part of your degree studies. Generally, if you take the four-year variant of a degree, it includes one year studying abroad in another country. This may sound daunting, but an extra year of study will not only give you the opportunity of working on your language skills (although many universities globally teach in English so language is not necessarily going to be an issue), but it will also potentially set your CV apart from others where there is no evidence of international experience. The possibility of earning a BA (Hons) English with a European placement, for example, might give you the edge you'd need to break into your desired career field.

Task – Make a list of the skills and expertise you would like to develop during your time at university. These might be related to your subject, or they might be something like learning a foreign language, learning to do basic web design, learning to drive or developing the confidence to travel solo to an exotic country. How might you go about gaining these skills? What sort of training might be needed? Is there any way the options you choose during your degree could offer the opportunity to develop these skills?

The first year doesn't really count, right?

There is a dangerous rumour going around that it really doesn't matter how well you do in your first year, as the marks don't count towards your final degree classification. Well – yes and no. You must pass the first year in order to progress onto the second, and obviously, the better you do in the first year when you're learning the ropes and setting up good study habits, the more likely you'll be aiming for a higher classification of degree by the end of your course. If you do not submit all of your assessments for the first year and don't manage to do these as resits, you will end up with marks of 'irretrievable deficit' – this means it is likely you will never be able to earn enough credits for a full honours degree. Avoid this at all costs; just try to get your work in on time – even if you feel it is not good enough, you need to submit something in order to earn the chance of a resit. If you choose to barely squeak through your first year, it will be exceedingly difficult to bring your study skills and attitudes up to a level that will ensure you a high level of academic success. My advice is to begin as you mean to go on.

For most universities in the UK, your marks in the second year are weighted at 30 per cent of your final degree classification, and your marks in the third year are weighted at 70 per cent – keep in mind that the final dissertation will form a large percentage of the final year's weighting, so clarify the details with your course leader.

Task – Find three students from your course: a first year, a second year and a third year. Ask them what they honestly wish they had known before they started their university course. You might be surprised at their candid answers!

ENGLISH LITERATURE: YEAR TWO
Devon Campbell-Hall

Introduction

This chapter gives you the advice you need to build on the skills learned in Year One. You will get lots of practical advice, including ideas on how to improve your academic writing, developing as an academic, how to maintain a good work–life balance and the importance of theory. You will be provided with practical tips on applying for work experience to aid your future career. There will also be lots of helpful comments from previous students.

What to Expect of the Second Year

What I loved most about my English degree was the broad range of texts we covered. There were endless lively debates and discussions on everything from the originality of the Grimm's tales to the social constructs in *Fight Club*. We were encouraged to develop our own interpretation of the texts, and taught how to express this in a structured context – thanks to one of my lecturers I will never forget how to PEE (point, evidence and explain). The techniques I learned helped me land a career in the communications department of the NHS. My degree gave me focus and I discovered my passion for writing, which I am now lucky enough to exercise through my career. It also taught me that with patience and determination, it is possible to read the entirety of *Bleak House* by Charles Dickens.

(Lizzie, graduate, (Hons) English and Magazine Journalism)

By the end of this section, you should have some idea of:

- how to move your academic writing on towards the next level of sophistication
- why understanding literary and cultural theory is so important
- how to become more academically independent
- how to decide on a dissertation topic
- how to balance your social life with the rigours of your academic life

Improving your academic writing

By the beginning of the second year of your degree course, you will have received feedback on perhaps half a dozen essays and numerous other types of assessments. If you haven't already done so, it is a good idea to ask your tutors if they have samples of successful pieces of work by former students. Carefully reading a selection of these whilst consulting the marking criteria in your unit handbook should clarify exactly the quality and style of work you'll need to produce in order to earn good marks. You might even ask your tutor if they could provide the seminar group with a marking grid and a selection of former students' essays without any marks for you to 'mock mark' in groups of three or four. Typically, students mark other students' work rather harshly – 10 per cent lower on average than the actual mark received. This is exceedingly useful for developing the skills of critical self-editing, so when you read through your own writing, your errors become glaringly obvious. This is one of the keys to producing better work: become a better self-editor.

The move from A-level to the first year of a degree necessarily challenges you to begin to write in a more academically sound manner. By now you will realize that there is no point simply rehashing your A-level essays in the hope they will pass at university level. They are likely to fail for a very good reason: *university essays are not about your personal opinion, but about how well you can organize and present the existing, published, scholarly ideas of current thinkers in order to lend weight to your own ideas.* Of course your opinion matters, but there is a process that needs to be followed in order to bring your opinion into the realm of scholarly debate.

Think of an essay as a case in the criminal courts. If the defence simply marched up to the podium and announced to the judge and jury that they believed the accused to be innocent and then sat down again, his/her proclamation would have no credibility. What is required is evidence, a clear line of reasoning and witnesses. When the defence makes a *point*, this clearly introduces an idea and leads the judge and jury through a logical line of reasoning. It is then necessary to introduce *evidence* – as we introduce scholarly quotes (from critical secondary sources such as journal articles, book chapters, etc.) within an essay – to support the argument. Finally, the argued line of reasoning is supported by bringing in *witnesses* – as we bring in brief examples from the primary texts (the novels, plays or poems we are writing about). Of course, the defence can't leave it at that – it is essential to explain clearly how the evidence and witness statements not only support their argument but move it to a new place. The goal is proving the innocence of the accused. Our goal as essay writers is to introduce our points, argue them logically using sound evidence to support our contentions, and then come to an intelligent conclusion *based on the evidence provided*. A-levels may teach us how to write a concise essay, but university teaches us to do so in an academic, watertight manner. One of the most important sets of tools we use to support our academic writing is critical, cultural or literary theory.

Task – Quickly read through one of the essays you wrote for A-level or for your first year of university studies. Gasp at the errors of judgement! Can you see how much your work has improved? Think how much it will have improved again by the end of your third year.

What is the point of theory?

Theory is a fancy word for the scholarly ideas of respected academics in a particular field. Theory provides new 'spectacles' through which we can consider the world around us. More importantly, theory can help us to understand how literature interacts with the cultural structures in which it was produced. It helps us to make sense of different points of view, and to read a single text in many different ways. My former colleague Dr Steve Purcell (now an associate professor of Shakespeare and performance studies at Warwick) and I came up with a useful metaphor for coming to terms with theory: the London Eye. The explanations that follow come directly from one of his clever introductory lectures. Each theoretical approach we consider is simply one 'perspective', just as each capsule on the London Eye provides a different view of the city. No single approach is necessarily better, more complete or more correct than any other, and you do not have to master all of the different approaches at once.

Let's begin by taking approaches that are 'close to the ground', just as if we're on the lowest level of the London Eye. Look around you – close up, we can examine the building just beneath us: its exterior surface, its brickwork, its decoration. *Close reading* does exactly what the name suggests: it pays close attention to the smallest details of a text. Why that specific word? Why that particular image? Why that word order? As we rise a little higher above the ground, our perspective begins to widen. Likewise, we can consider *form, narrative and genre* within a text. The small details may be reflected in the wider structures surrounding them: the shape of a building as a whole, or even the location of a building within a street. In the same way, the details of a text will make up part of a bigger picture: they may reflect, support or even subvert the shape of the narrative or the conventions of the genre.

If we go higher still, we notice other features of the cityscape. Here we begin to see that our building is not simply remarkable in and of itself; it is also interesting because of the way it fits (or doesn't quite fit) into the city around it. *Critical, cultural and literary theory* can in a similar way help us to understand how a text fits into other texts within the literary canon; they are interesting because of how they relate to each other, as well as through their own literary merit. As we reach the top of the London Eye, our perspective grows wider yet and we gain a sense of the building's context within Central and even Greater London. Likewise, theory can help us contextualize works of literature: we can begin to see how they might reflect, support or subvert the values of the cultures for which they were produced. Of course, this perspective cannot remain static.

As we come down on the other side of the London Eye, we have gained a wider sense of the various 'perspectives' on offer. Using quotes from theory to support our arguments in essays likewise allows us to understand and make sense of different points of view. It doesn't mean these are our own personal points of view, but it does mean we can understand how to read a text through these 'spectacles'.

Task – Make a list of the various 'lenses' through which you view the world. How might you see a current event – say the implementation of higher fees for university study – through these various viewpoints? How might your opinions differ, depending on your vantage point?

Reaching towards academic independence

Along with your growing sense of how to use theory to write a strong academic essay, you should make a point of trying to become less dependent upon your lecturers to guide you every step of the way. They are there to support, help, teach and guide, but it is not their job to hold your hand throughout your degree studies. Your lecturers are not your drinking buddies. They are not your Facebook friends. They are the beastly monsters whose job it is to challenge you to reach your academic best. You may not always like them and they may not always like you, but it is their job to introduce you to new ideas, new possibilities and new ways of looking at the world. Learning is not always enjoyable: it can be painful, awkward and may bring you to tears, but the point of the exercise is to help you to become an independent scholar who is self-motivated to produce excellent work that is turned in on time. This doesn't happen automatically, though – it comes over time after you've fully participated in all of the teaching and learning activities your course provides. This means attending all of the lectures, preparing well for all of the seminars, going to the guest lectures, meeting with your fellow students for study sessions, and most importantly, spending enough time on your independent studies and individual reading. Get in the habit of reading your work aloud to yourself – any quirks in your writing style will quickly become obvious. This will become particularly important as you begin to think about your *final year project*, also called a *dissertation*. Keep in mind that not all higher education institutions require a dissertation, but it is generally the difference between, for example, a degree of English (ordinary degree) and (Hons) English (honours degree). Alternatives might include the possibility, for example, of submitting original creative work underpinned by a related short, critical piece of supportive analytical writing. In the past, my own students have submitted original work such as poetry collections, theatrical play scripts, screenplays, the design/pilot copy of a new literary magazine, an advertising campaign for literacy awareness, and short films. Finally, there is the choice to be examined by oral viva rather than by written exam. Some other universities offer the option to do a shorter final project / mini-dissertation for less credit, plus a combination of taught modules culminating in coursework or final exams. Still others might allow students to dispense with the dissertation altogether and make up their final year purely from taught modules. Consider your options carefully and play to your own strengths. If a student successfully completes all taught components and assessments for their undergraduate degree except for the dissertation, they may well opt to leave with their ordinary degree and avoid the extra stress of the final project. Do check with your institution as to their specific requirements. Remember, though, that many employers require an a honours degree, and you may well be called upon to justify your choice to leave with an ordinary, unclassified degree, which may affect your job prospects.

Choosing a dissertation topic

So what is this dissertation, and how can students generate and define their ideas to ensure the greatest possibility of academic success? The dissertation will be your magnum opus, the pinnacle of your career as a university student. You choose your topic in the second year, but produce the work in your third year. The first deadline tends to be in the November of the third year, thus the need to clarify what you hope to do months beforehand. It may sound like the distant future, but this deadline comes around very, very quickly.

Students of English generally have the option of either doing a traditional 10,000 word critical academic dissertation or a creative/practical project with a strong element of academic underpinning. Some students write novellas, some create portfolios of original epic poetry; others may decide to create a literary magazine or a literary feature for a local newspaper. Different institutions obviously have different regulations that will determine the freedom you will have in choosing the sort of dissertation you will write, so you must check these very carefully with your course leader.

You will probably be asked to write a brief overview of the sort of project you have in mind before the spring break of the second year of your degree course. This allows the dissertation coordinator to assess the viability of your proposed project and to find an appropriate supervisor with sound knowledge of your proposed area of study. Your supervisor may come from within the English faculty, or in the case of joint honours degrees, they may well come from within the joint honours faculty. What is essential is that you keep the line of communication open between you and your supervisor, so you are clear about deadlines and exactly what is expected of you.

During the first term of your second year, it is a good idea to start thinking of possible areas of study. Although generally English literature dissertations focus on poetry, prose or dramatic works, you may want to explore tangentially related aspects of literary production or the literary industry. For students of the English language, the rich world of linguistics is open to you – you can consider various aspects of dialect, accent, world Englishes, etc. It is wise to choose a subject likely to hold your interest for the long haul, as writing a dissertation will take up most of your third year of study.

Task – Brainstorm a quick list of your ideal dissertation topics. Don't worry about their 'appropriateness' at this stage – just scribble down those dream topics you feel could hold your attention through months of gruelling research and writing. Now consider the list – how could you take these rough ideas and turn them into something viable for a student of English? Which of these might prove the most practical towards your future career? Which of these might you want to study much more deeply as a postgraduate?

Achieving the work–life balance

During their second year at university, most students find it tough to survive on their maintenance grant alone, so many take on part-time jobs to supplement their meagre income. If you are an organized sort of person with few vices, this can be successful. However, if your goal of working is more about earning enough money for boozy weekends than it is about gaining valuable work experience that may help your future career, you may want to think twice before taking on more than ten hours' outside work per week. The prospect of earning a few hundred pounds can seem more enticing than hauling yourself out of bed to go to yet another lecture, but it is all too easy to fall into bad habits that can have long-term negative effects on your academic success. By all means party hard with your pals, but not until you've finished writing that essay or preparing that presentation.

Interestingly, the students who tend to finish up with the best degrees tend not to be the brilliant high-flyers who breeze in on their laurels with a stunning natural intellect, but those students who modestly plod along, determined to succeed. These are the good attenders whose work is never late, who participate in all of the course events, and who read and reread, write and rewrite. Not surprisingly, they tend also to be those students who listen to their lecturers and take on board their suggestions for improving their work. Ahem.

Developing as an Academic and Beyond

On my English and Media degree programme, I had the chance to improve my English, as I am an international student. I learnt how to be thorough, how to work hard and never take anything for granted. The course also helped me to grow up and think independently. The most important thing is that I am now following my dream of studying for a master's degree in journalism in New York. My work experience is at the *New York Times* – and the uni is just across the road from the UN building. All this from an English degree!

(Marianne, graduate, BA (Hons) English and Media)

By the end of this section, you should have some idea of:

- how to network successfully

- why it is not too early to think about your future career

- how to find work experience

- how you can prepare yourself for a career in teaching

- the options for postgraduate study

Networking

In addition to developing academically and hopefully maintaining a strong academic performance on all of your assessments, this is the time you need to begin making contacts that will form your professional network once you graduate. There are a few things you'll need to think about before you can begin: your area of expertise, your skills, networking opportunities, and how you'll market yourself as a potential employee. How can you possibly know in your second year of university what your specialization will be? You may not have the slightest idea by now, or there may be some aspect of your course that has proven truly inspirational. It may be Elizabethan theatre, learning how to organize a literature festival or working on the editorial team for your in-house student literary journal. Whatever your pleasure, you need to be sure to develop clear knowledge and concrete skills within these areas. If you know what you *love*, what you *can* do and what you *would like* to do, you will be ready to think about how you might come across like-minded people who already work in these fields. You may meet people at public lectures, specialist workshops, in bookshops, while on work experience or through professional social networking sites such as LinkedIn. The next step is to make sure they remember you – this does not mean perfecting your tap dance routine. This does mean working out what information to give out to relative strangers so you stay safe but so they might contact you if any opportunities arise. My suggestion is to have some simple business cards made up. There are several online companies who will print business cards for free (but with their logo on the back) if you'll pay the postage. These are a good option to start with. I would recommend your name, the degree course you are taking, your areas of developing specialization and an e-mail contact address and mobile number. I do not recommend a landline number or a permanent address at this stage. Now all you need to do is get yourself to some events, swallow your fear and get networking!

Task – Design your new business card. Think of the format, the text and what you want this card to say about you as a potential employee/contact. Design something others will want to keep for future reference.

Start thinking about your career

It is not too early to begin really thinking about the career you would like to pursue after graduation. If you have no idea where to begin, start with your university's career centre, and book yourself in for a one-to-one session with an expert, who can quickly help you to work out the sorts of jobs that might suit your temperament, skills and preferences. If you are still stuck, think about the sorts of environments in which you are the happiest – quiet, noisy, busy, private, inside, outside, with animals, with children, with lots of stress, etc. Could you imagine yourself working in such an environment for eight hours a day? Do you prefer working in groups, on your own, or a combination of the two? Do you prefer writing or speaking? Coming up with answers to these questions will help you to hone your ideas of the sorts of jobs that might naturally suit you. Here your growing skills in networking really become useful – when you meet someone who clearly loves their job, ask them about it. How did they get into their field? Which qualifications were required? Do they have any work experience opportunities coming up? Of course this is difficult and embarrassing and awkward, but practice definitely helps to build confidence in your ability to speak to relative strangers about their careers.

What you must keep in mind is that regardless of your level of education, when you begin a new job (particularly when you have little or no job experience behind you), you start at the bottom of the ladder. With the right degree, the right attitude and the right performance, you are likely to move up quickly, but don't make the mistake of thinking the world owes you a good job just because you will soon be a graduate. There are always more people looking for jobs than there are jobs to go around, and competition is fierce. Your task is to make yourself attractive as a potential employee. One of the best ways to do this is to ensure that throughout your degree studies, you are gaining valuable work experience.

Finding work experience

Many of the best jobs are never advertised – they might not even exist until some bright spark identifies a 'problem' within an organization that they can solve. Thus many of the most exciting careers are born. In a similar way, many of the best work experience opportunities are not advertised, but come either through word of mouth through your personal network, or you can 'create' such opportunities yourself. In the current economic climate, it is rare for someone to land a fabulous job without solid work experience behind them. A good degree is no longer enough on its own; you must have evidence to support your contention that you are the 'best person for the job'. Finding a good work experience placement is often the key to success. Your university careers centre will certainly have a database list of many local opportunities, but these will be exceedingly oversubscribed. Your best bet is to use your contacts, and to pound the pavement! There is no point waiting around to see if anyone contacts you – contact them first! By all means list yourself on such sites as Graduate Jobs South, but try to be proactive. Most work experience placements will be unpaid, but it is still essential to be punctual, professional and properly dressed for the job. Treat it as if it were the real thing, and who knows, you might be offered something permanent as a result. Be sure to get a good reference from your work experience provider, and do ask if they would be willing to be a referee for your CV.

Task – Make a list of all of the job contacts you have through family and friends. Now think outside this box – how about through friends of friends or local social groups? What sorts of work do those closest to you do? Can you imagine any role for you as a new English graduate in their companies?

If you hope to become a teacher

> No one in my family thinks I have what it takes to be a teacher, but my lecturer believes in me. She pushed me to reach towards my dreams and got tough with me when she saw me nearly giving up. I can't believe I made it through my degree – and I'm now working with kids who've been excluded from school, to help them to get back into the system and reach their potential, the same way my lecturer helped me to reach mine. Who'd have thought this Essex party boy could make such a difference to kids' lives?
>
> (Patrick, graduate, BA (Hons) English and Media)

Teaching is certainly one of the most intoxicating – and exasperating – careers on the planet, but I wouldn't want to do anything else. Once I started teaching, I realized I was likely to spontaneously combust if I didn't continue. If you think this may be the right job for you, you would be wise to gain experience working in schools during your second and third year of university. Before applying for the one-year PGCE course (the UK qualification leading to qualified teacher status) you will need an absolute minimum of two weeks' work experience in a school environment at the level at which you wish you teach. This is to weed out those whom teaching really would not suit. Either you'll love the challenge or you'll run for the hills after the first day. The reason I suggest you begin in your second year of university is that everyone will have two weeks' experience – if you can manage several months' worth, all the better. Head teachers receive dozens of requests each term for such experience, so again, this is the time to use those contacts I've been on about. Call the head from your primary school, your secondary school or your college to see if they might welcome you in for such an opportunity. You will have to be persistent, as the schools are actually doing you a favour and this makes more work for their teaching staff.

Options for postgraduate study

If the prospect of doing further study at master's degree level after graduation appeals to you, keep in mind that you'll need to earn at least a 2:1 (upper second) degree, which equates to a B. At present, there is very little funding for master's-level study, which puts most students off immediately. However, if you simply must carry on and know you can't afford it, there are ways and means. If your savings have run dry and no maiden aunts come forth with offers to fund your passion for further study, you can always do it one of two ways: work part time and study part time over two or three years, or spend weeks in the local library poring over that wonderfully weighty tome, *The Grants Register*. Most libraries will have a copy of this in their reference section, but it can't be checked out so you'll need to do your research in the library. There are literally thousands of small bursaries and scholarships (from £25 to £500) that are unclaimed each year because no one bothers to apply. This may be due to the long, laborious process – you often need to apply at least a year in advance, write a long essay, give a presentation and agree to appear in the group's marketing materials. The sheer effort and hassle involved puts most people off, but if you crave postgraduate studies at a cellular level, this is one way of making it happen. If you add together enough pots of £75, you will eventually have enough for tuition fees! You may even do it the old-fashioned way – work hard and save up until you have enough to take a year out of full-time employment to pursue your dream course. Some employers are willing to partially fund master's degree courses, if you can demonstrate your increased value to the company.

Task – Make a list of those areas of your degree studies you are enjoying most. Would you consider doing a postgraduate degree to study any of these in more depth?

ENGLISH LITERATURE: YEAR THREE
Devon Campbell-Hall

Introduction

Congratulations on getting to Year Three. This chapter will help you to prepare and complete the final year of your degree programme. You will gain an understanding of degree classifications and how to do damage limitation if you've missed work, or are struggling with workload. In addition, you will consider the importance of deadlines and planning ahead, especially now. You'll also get advice on how to fine-tune your dissertation and tips on structuring and polishing it.

Achieving the Degree You Want

> The best thing about the course overall is changing your opinion of the way you see things, and the way you think about things. I've changed so much in three years. Doing this degree has given me confidence by learning to give presentations. You don't just learn about English, you learn about history and culture and you learn to look at things in a totally different way. It develops you completely.
>
> (Ariana, graduate, BA (Hons) English and
> Writing Contemporary Fiction)

By the end of this section, you should have some idea of:

* what degree classifications mean

* why deadlines matter

- how to repair a patchy academic record

- what third-year tutors are really looking for in your written assessments

- how to give successful presentations for the best marks

- the role of internships

- how to use social networking to grow your professional image

- how to begin the long job hunt long before graduation

Degree classifications

If you complete the 360 CATS (credit accumulation and transfer scheme) points needed to earn your honours degree (keeping in mind that most undergraduate units are worth 20 CATS points), your degree will be graded according to whatever classification system is in use. This periodically undergoes change to reflect current thinking. Currently, degrees are classified as follows: 1st (the tops – A), 2:1 (B), 2:2 (C) or 3rd (just made it through with a D). If you are planning on pursuing postgraduate studies, you'll really need to be aiming for the equivalent of a 1st or 2:1. If you are planning on applying for scholarships or funding to support your further studies, a 1st will be essential. Remember, a 2:2 is the average mark, and 1sts are rare. There are also unclassified or ordinary degrees, which imply that you did your studies and completed everything except for the final year dissertation. It is a very good idea to push yourself to get a classified honours degree, as you would be hard pushed to carry on academically without one.

Deadlines

Have I mentioned how important it is to be sure to get your work done properly and on time? Er, yes – numerous times! It is good practice to develop the discipline of turning in your work a bit before the deadline. There is a solid reason for this: consistently turning in work late means consistently reduced marks which means a much lower eventual degree classification than you deserve! Pull the cork out and get on with it – the consequences of habitually late work are serious and generally avoidable. In the case of medical emergencies, the death of a very close family member (I say 'very close' only because it is extraordinary how many grandmothers and great uncles seem to pass away just before an essay deadline looms) or some other catastrophe, you can always apply for extenuating circumstances. This means that you are not 'fit to sit' an assessment.

If your circumstances with accompanying evidence are indeed accepted, then you should be granted the opportunity to submit your work over the summer, without the marks being capped. If, however, your circumstances are not accepted as 'extenuating', you will most likely just be offered a resit with the marks capped at the lowest passing mark (usually 40 per cent).

University deadlines are a good preparation for the sorts of deadlines we will all face in a working environment, but in an employment situation, a habitual lack of punctuality may mean you lose your job! Keep in mind also that even if you do not pass a unit, you are still responsible for the full fees, so if you are not careful, you may end up with three years of student debt and nothing to show for it. Employers continually tell academics that some of the most important job skills are what we might call 'soft skills': punctuality, politeness, courtesy, the ability to think independently, the ability to take direction, the ability to work with minimal supervision, the ability to write correctly and intelligently, the ability to speak well ... and *the ability to get work done on time and to a good standard*. Need I say more on this?

Damage limitation

If you find yourself in the unfortunate situation of knowing full well you have failed to complete all of the necessary assessments to pass particular units, do not give up hope! You may need to give up your dream of a 1st or 2:1 (or even a 2:2, if you have missed quite a few bits of work), but there may still be a chance for you to earn a 3rd or even an unclassified degree. These are not ideal, but they are certainly better than throwing away the entire chance of earning a university degree! Rather than burying your head in the sand, *contact your course leader*. They are likely to be supportive of your situation if they can detect genuine remorse and a sincere desire to sort yourself out. You will not have been the first student in history to get yourself into a mess, but you are the only one who can get yourself out. It may be best for you to suspend your studies for a year or more – this means you 'stop the clock' to take stock of what you really want, with the full intention of coming back later to try again. In order to do this, you must apply formally through your faculty office so you are not liable for even more fees! If all else fails, you'll want to be sure to at least earn a diploma of higher education or a certificate of higher education; not ideal, but at least these would acknowledge some of your efforts towards degree-level studies. If you decide to try again in the future, these may allow you to transfer on to another degree course in the second – or even the third – year.

Task – Contact the course support team in your faculty office to find out the exact state of play with your academic record. If you

have missed any assessment deadlines, find out exactly what your options are for resits. Are you still on target for a full honours degree? Ignorance is not bliss here, but time is of the essence.

What tutors really want from their students

Tutors want their students to succeed. Period. This means attending all scheduled teaching events, preparing well for sessions, doing all of the readings in advance and ensuring that you spend a good two or three hours in the library reading in preparation for each teaching event. It's really rather simple: we want you to learn to behave in the positive, professional manner you will need to behave in in order to succeed in the working world. At this level of your studies, tutors will expect you to not only read the novel/poems/plays for a particular week's lessons, but also to have read several academic articles or book chapters around the texts, as well as supportive material that will help you to understand the context in which a text was created.

You will be offered regular one-on-one tutorials with your unit leaders, but it is always your responsibility to sign up for these (usually on the tutor's door or via the faculty office) and to turn up on time. Find out how much tutorial time you are entitled to, and be sure to avail yourself of these valuable support/learning opportunities for each of your units. Some tutors are willing to read through drafts of essays and projects, but others prefer to see only essay plans; find out what your tutors prefer. If they refuse to read drafts, do not be offended – this is simply another opportunity for you to learn to become more academically independent. For in-depth essay guidance, you can sign up for essay writing sessions through the university library, or consult the electronic resources on your university's virtual learning environment. This amazing virtual learning space provides opportunities to develop your essay writing skills, your employability skills, and even helps you learn how to give better presentations, one of the most useful forms of assessment during your third year.

Great presentations

If you are naturally shy and loathe public speaking, the prospect of having to give an assessed presentation may seem like an insurmountable barrier to your success. Never fear – there are some techniques that might help you to gain the confidence necessary to give a great presentation that leaves your audience informed, interested and wanting more. First of all, remember that everyone in your seminar group will be in the same boat – many of your student colleagues will share your dread of speaking to a group of their peers. Secondly, remember that your tutor may appear to be an exceedingly confident and knowledgeable speaker, but it is very likely they, too, struggled with the process when they began. The first thing to sort out is to clarify exactly the subject on which you are to present. Your tutor may assign particular topics on specific texts, or they may leave the option open for you to choose your own area of discussion that contends with some aspect of the texts you're all studying on a particular unit. Plan the presentation in the same way you'd begin to plan an essay; an introduction, three or four main points and a conclusion. You may choose to present using tools such as PowerPoint or Prezi, or you may prefer to simply speak the old-fashioned way with a few index cards with notes. What never works is reading directly from either notes or slides. By all means refer to your slides to emphasize key points, but do not simply regurgitate line upon line of tedious quoted text from a slide. I personally find it much more useful to use slides as an aide-memoire − I find that if my slides consist largely of relevant images that trigger my memory as to the points I plan to cover, I give much better presentations. This is also much better for the audience.

Third-year presentations are generally around fifteen to twenty minutes. Allow at least three to five minutes for questions − if no one asks any, prompt them! If your tutor offers the opportunity to lead a seminar discussion (non-assessed), this is a terrific opportunity to hone your skills. Ask your fellow students and the tutor for feedback, and use this to improve your presentation for the actual assessed version. Handouts are a good idea, as long as they are interesting, relevant and useful. I find that after the first ten minutes of a presentation, I like to introduce a short group activity that gets people talking and working together. This also breaks any tedium.

In a nutshell, a good format to consider is this: 1) introduce the topic − tell your audience what you're going to tell them; 2) make your points, supporting them with appropriate evidence, and always linking them together logically from one point to the next; 3) introduce a short group activity that gets the audience to discuss some of the ideas you've presented in a practical way; 4) conclude the presentation by bringing together everything you've discussed − remind the audience what you've told them, and then open the floor to questions. Most importantly, keep your voice modulated and calm, but never monotonous. What sort of presenter do you enjoy listening to? Enthusiastic? Knowledgeable? Amusing?

Task − Consider the last really good presentation you heard. What about it worked well? How could the presenter have improved their performance? Make a list of the terrific presentation skills you want to develop.

Internships

In Year Two, we discussed techniques for finding work experience. Internships are also work experience, but many (not all) are paid and they are generally for either a summer or a full year, with the possibility of a full-time job in the end if it goes well. Keep in mind that in many industries, it is nearly impossible to get an interview for a full-time job until you have successfully completed an unpaid internship first to learn the ropes.

You must treat internships as if they are a probationary period for a full-time job, and demonstrate full commitment to the opportunity. Competition is fierce – you will be interviewed either by phone or in person. Modern interviews tend to be competency based rather than knowledge based, so you need to think about your skills and abilities before the big day. It is wise to make a mind map of accomplishments you are proud of before the interview, as this may well come up. Ask a close friend or family member to do the same, and compare notes – you may well be surprised at what they have noticed about you and your strengths! These need not necessarily be academic or professional achievements, but anything you have accomplished personally that took guts, determination and endurance. Ask your tutors if they would consider giving you a mock interview so you can work on your techniques, and be sure to ask for feedback to improve your performance. Practice makes perfect.

In the unlikely event you are not successful in getting an internship, do swallow your pride and ask for feedback from those who interviewed you. They will only give it if you ask, and this will prove invaluable for building your skills for the next time.

Social networking

In this day of online social networking, privacy is rapidly becoming an outdated notion. My advice has always been to only post information, photos, comments and ideas onto e-mail systems or social networking sites if you would be happy for your mother, grandmother, spiritual leader, dean of faculty, neighbour or ex-partner to read and disseminate them freely. Messages easily get 'accidentally' forwarded on to other parties, and we must be vigilant in editing what we launch into cyberspace. Now is the time to begin to edit your Facebook profile to remove those compromising photos and questionable comments, before a potential employer sees them and makes a snap judgement regarding your character and suitability for a position. Put all of the privacy settings in place, but realize that any decent techno-wizard with a bit of time and determination can probably break through these with some ease. The best advice is to think of every wall post as a potential tool of self-marketing towards your future career.

Amongst the many positive uses for social networking are finding out about internship and job opportunities, scholarships for further study, writing competitions, study abroad opportunities and, of course, for connecting with like-minded people who share your passions for obscure works of literature. Be careful and think before you press the 'post' button.

Task – If you have not already done so, create a LinkedIn profile. Ask your tutors to connect with you; this is a wonderful way of getting them to write sparkling references you can actually see.

The job hunt

When you are writing up your dissertation and being sure to properly prepare for any upcoming final exams, the last thing on your mind may be the future job hunt. Keep in mind that it is wise to get into the habit of scanning the broadsheets for job opportunities every week, even if you're not yet in the zone for seriously looking. This will keep you informed about the sorts of jobs out there, the sorts of qualifications and experience they are looking for, and the sorts of possible salaries you might be looking at. Remember, competition is always fierce, so you need to set your application, CV and cover letter apart from the rest. Make an appointment with the careers centre at your university to go through your CV and to book a mock interview with an advisor. They can help you highlight those areas needing attention and improvement before you begin the serious search for that perfect job. All of the advice suggested so far in the chapters on Years One, Two and Three is leading you up to this point: preparing you for the exciting path ahead. You will be spending a large proportion of your intellectual energies during this final year of your studies writing and editing that magnum opus, your masterwork – the dissertation.

The Dissertation

I never thought I'd say this, but I have really loved my final year and through the process of writing my FYP and revising for the exam, I have experienced enormous personal growth and focus. Thank you for encouraging me to see it all through.

(Karen, BA (Hons) English and Professional Writing)

By the end of this section, you should have some idea of:

• the importance of your final year project / dissertation

• the dissertation time frame

- fine-tuning your topic

- organizing your research

- how to structure the dissertation

- how to get the best out of your supervisor / personal tutor

- how to produce a dissertation that showcases your best work

- what to do with your dissertation after graduation

The majority of English degrees offer students the opportunity to undertake a dissertation during the final year of their degree course. This is what differentiates an honours degree (i.e., BA (Hons) English) from an ordinary degree (i.e., BA English). Successfully completing and passing the dissertation is one of the final hurdles of degree-level study, and it is probably the assessment that students find the most stressful. Many students do not appreciate the depth of analysis and length of time required to complete the dissertation, and thus, they leave the writing up until the last minute. Remember, this final project is more heavily weighted than anything else you've written throughout your degree, so it pays to do a fabulous job. This chapter aims to demystify the dissertation process, by clarifying exactly what will be expected of you and suggesting an appropriate time frame for the various 'hoops' you'll need to jump through. Finally, it will offer tips on how to collate and shape your research, as well as advice on how to structure, write and polish the final dissertation.

Time frame

The reason it is crucial to start thinking about your dissertation topic during your second year is that the first deadline will come up very, very soon after you begin your third year, and it takes time to form the ideas necessary – let alone to ensure you have read all of the primary texts to support your ideas – for writing a great piece of work. The first deadline for dissertations (usually around 2,000 words, but it varies) tends to be around the end of November of your third year of study. This often takes the form of a 'pitch' or an introduction to the project, including a short literature review and a brief overview of your proposed methodology for the project. You will have numerous one-to-one tutorial sessions with your supervisor throughout the dissertation process, and you will discuss and decide upon deadlines together for various parts of the final project. Generally, the dissertation (usually around 10,000 words total) is to be completed and handed in for assessment in late April or early May of your final year of study, to allow it to be marked, second marked and then externally marked before the summer exam boards. Your course leader will clarify exactly the format the dissertation is to take – usually it is to be double-spaced, in an easy-to-read font such as Times New Roman, in 12 point size. You usually hand in two bound copies (either wire- or spiral-bound, depending on your institution). It is your responsibility to make tutorial appointments with your supervisor – it is not their job to chase you. You will need to negotiate how often you will meet, and if you need to send work electronically beforehand. These sessions are an essential aspect of the dissertation process, and it would be very tough to create a good piece of work at this high level without their tough critical support. They may well 'tighten the thumb screws' if they feel you are faffing around and working too slowly, but in the end, you will call the shots.

Task – Make a list of your favourite procrastination techniques. How can you remove the temptation to fall into these when deadlines loom? Think of some of the ways you could reward yourself for meeting deadlines or even getting work in early.

Fine-tuning your topic

Many students panic at the prospect of having to write a 10,000-word dissertation on a single subject. When you are used to writing 2,500-word essays, this might seem a daunting leap. Consider this – these 10,000 words are rather like five 2,000-word essays, all on related but varied aspects of a specific subject, all sharing a logical, common thread that leads you towards a magnificent conclusion. Broken down into manageable chunks, it makes more sense. The first 2,000 words are likely to consist of, at least in part, the introduction / project overview / pitch you submitted back in the autumn of this academic year. When you receive feedback and the grade mark for this piece of work, you will have a much clearer idea of its viability as a project, and whether or not you are on the right track. This is of course why we ask you to submit your proposed title before the end of the second year of your studies – so an appropriate supervisor can be identified, and so you can begin to converse with them about the practicalities of your project.

Most students begin with a topic that is far too large and wide ranging for an undergraduate dissertation. For example, one of my students was interested in writing about 'Prostitution in Literature', which was of course far too big a subject. We began to narrow the subject down to 'Representations of Prostitution in Early Novels in English', but as this was still rather too broad a topic, it became 'Representations of Prostitution in Daniel Defoe's *Moll Flanders* and John Cleland's *Fanny Hill*'. What was lacking here was the main area of interest for the project – what was interesting about these representations? What did the project aim to do? Her eventual title became 'Comparing Representations of the Motivations for Entering Prostitution within *Moll Flanders* and *Fanny Hill*'. From this streamlined title, the student managed to write an outstanding dissertation with excellent, logical structure and well-supported arguments. It earned a 1st.

Organizing your research

Everyone has their preferred method of keeping the chaos of research notes in some sort of order. Some prefer index cards in a neat file, with each topic in alphabetical order, while others prefer a separate small notebook for quotes from each of the important secondary texts you're consulting to support your work. Some students find it best to keep notes via a digital voice recorder. What is absolutely essential is that you keep a full critical record of all of your references of every single quote you will use. There is little more demoralizing than spending the entire day before submitting your dissertation in the library, desperately trying to find a page number for an obscure reference! Don't be tempted to make these up – your tutor will probably have read nearly all of the books from which you're quoting, and it is exceedingly embarrassing to be caught out. Also, most dissertations are now submitted electronically via tools such as Turnitin, which serve as plagiarism detection tools. Keep good notes and decide in advance how you will keep these in some semblance of order so you can later find the quotes you need when you need them.

You may find that using programmes such as endnotes or other research/ bibliographic tools is useful for helping you to keep electronic records of your researched information. Book a training session with your IT department at the university to find out the tools available to you via the university portal. These could save you valuable time and much effort in the long run.

Structure

One of my students described a dissertation as 'an essay on steroids' – although I can see their point, a dissertation is so much more than simply the sum of its parts. It becomes the highlight of your academic production as an undergraduate – not because you are introducing altogether new, groundbreaking research, but because you are presenting a solid topic and managing to sustain this in-depth study over many months to a successful conclusion.

For a typical 10,000-word dissertation, I have found it helpful to consider this rough structure:

Introduction: including a literature review and methodological overview (2,000 words), leading logically into:

Chapter One: an essay that breaks down main point #1 into four separate points (2,000 words), leading logically into:

Chapter Two: an essay that breaks down main point #2 into four separate points (2,000 words), leading logically into:

Chapter Three: an essay that breaks down main point #3 into four separate points (2,000 words), leading logically into:

Conclusion: an overview of the points introduced in the previous chapters and clearly brings these threads together into a logical conclusion (2,000 words)

Do keep in mind that the three main chapters must all flow together to form a coherent whole. Your introduction, as with the essay guidance I offered in the section on Year Two, must introduce all of the primary texts you'll be discussing as well as giving the reader an idea of the sorts of trajectories you will take. Just give a rough idea of the sorts of areas you'll be discussing, and a clear indication of the methodology (i.e., the tools of theory or the 'spectacles') you will use to accomplish your goals within the project. Finally, the introduction should include a literature review, also known as a tangential literature search of relevant works already done on your subject and the main conclusions drawn by other scholars on this topic. Why? How can you possibly work out if your contribution will be interesting and somewhat original if you have not previously spent some time and effort finding out what has already been written about the subject? Your job is not to write a dissertation that is wholly new and original, but it is important that you evidence your familiarity with what has already been written about your topic, so you can show that you have a new way of 'reading' it. This can pave the way towards postgraduate studies, if you can identify an under-researched area that captures your interest. The most important thing to remember at this stage is there will be no substitute for regular tutorial sessions with your supervisor. They will help you to stay focused, keep on the right track and avoid the inevitable distractions that might keep you from successfully completing this project on time.

Getting the best out of your dissertation supervisor

Dissertation supervisors come in all shapes and sizes, so it will be your responsibility to determine how to get the best out of them. You must set the tone for the process – you can let them know how often you'd like to meet (usually it is every two weeks or so) and how much 'guidance' you prefer. Some students like to be left alone to get on with their research, while others prefer to be led by the hand through the early stages of the process. Be clear and try to articulate your needs so your supervisor can respond appropriately. If you are genuinely uncomfortable working with someone in particular, do discreetly ask the faculty office for a change of supervisor. This may or may not be possible, depending on the research expertise of the other staff members, but it is worth a try. You both need to be comfortable with the situation, as you'll be working closely together for several months. Communication is the key – find out exactly what your supervisor expects from you and vice versa, particularly when it comes to how/when to contact them with questions.

Task – Be sure to keep a clear record of exactly what is discussed and decided upon by you and your supervisor at each tutorial. Refer to this regularly to be sure you stay focused.

Polishing your dissertation to showcase your best work

By the time you've slaved for months writing up your dissertation, the prospect of editing and re-editing your work may seem intolerable. Try to finish it up at least one or two weeks in advance, so you can leave it for a few days. When you come back to read it through renewed, rested eyes, it will be shocking how many typographical errors and peculiarly structured sentences jump out! Read your work aloud and ask a trusted, details-oriented friend to read it over too, as sometimes we miss the mistakes in our own writing.

Find out exactly how your department requires dissertations to be presented – I prefer double-spacing and wide margins to allow plenty of space for tutor feedback comments. They may require two hard copies as well as one electronic copy. Be sure to include page numbers, a full table of contents and a full bibliography in the correct format for your department. We might be tempted to think that the greatest writers in history simply sat down and penned their masterpieces with no crossings-out, rewording or rehashing, but this is not possible. We all need to edit, edit, edit and rewrite, rewrite, rewrite our work to ensure it is polished and clear. Failing to properly proofread a dissertation may keep you from earning the mark you deserve.

What can I do with a dissertation after graduation?

If you have followed the advice and suggestions within this guide, it is likely you have chosen a dissertation topic that is in some way related to your career aspirations. For example, if you hope to become a primary school teacher, it might be wise to consider writing a dissertation on children's literature, or if you hope to break into publishing, it might be sensible to consider the publishing history of Shakespeare's comedies. If you decided to produce a creative, practical dissertation that combined practical writing with academic writing, you will probably have a fantastic piece of work to show future employers the sorts of things you're capable of producing. Don't make the mistake of assuming a dissertation that earns a first-class mark is ready to send to a potential editor. Anything you plan on trying to publish must make it through many hurdles before it could even be considered! There are numerous online student journals that might be good places to begin your search for a publishing opportunity. You might also consider submitting an abstract to a student conference, if the subject of the conference is one related to your new expertise. The key is to be sensible about what you have achieved. If it is truly outstanding and with real potential, your supervisor will tell you so.

Task – If your dissertation earned a first-class mark, aspects of it might have the potential to form the basis of a publishable article. Do some research into online academic journals that peer review student work for possible publication. Find out exactly what they are looking for and submit an abstract for their consideration.

Conclusion

I hope that you have found this a helpful guide to your studies and that it will enable you to get the most out of your degree programme – before, during and after. English literature creates some of the most dynamic, creative and analytical graduates whose skills are thoroughly valued in the workplace. Just remember, you get out what you put in! I wish you luck and success in both your degree and your future career.

BIBLIOGRAPHY

Ashcroft, Bill, Gareth Griffiths and Helen Tiffin, eds. 1993. *The Empire Writes Back*. London: Routledge.

Baldick, Chris. 2001. *Concise Dictionary of Literary Terms*. Oxford: Oxford University Press.

Barry, Peter. 2002. *Beginning Theory*. Manchester: Manchester University Press.

Carroll, Lewis. 1871. *Through the Looking-Glass and What Alice Found There*. London: Macmillan.

Eaglestone, Robert. 2002. *Doing English: A Guide for Literature Students*. London: Routledge.

Mounsey, Chris. 2002. *One Step Ahead: Essays and Dissertations*. Oxford: Oxford University Press.

Palgrave Macmillan. 2012. *The Grants Register: The Complete Guide to Postgraduate Funding Worldwide*. Basingstoke: Palgrave Macmillan.

Philips, C. H., ed. 1977. *The Correspondence of Lord William Cavendish Bentinck, Governor-General of India, 1828–1835*, vol. 2. Oxford: Oxford University Press.

Sarnowski, Joe. 2014. 'The Process Is the Product'. Online: http://www.sdcc.edu/uploadedFiles/SDCCedu/Academics/Faculty/Sarnowski.pdf (accessed 5 May).

Waugh, Evelyn. 1945. *Brideshead Revisited*. London: Chapman and Hall.

Online Resources

Academic OneFile. http://www.gale.cengage.com/PeriodicalSolutions/academicOnefile.htm (accessed 26 May 2014).

English Subject Centre (Higher Education Academy). 2014. *Why Study English?* http://www.whystudyenglish.ac.uk (accessed 26 May 2014).

JSTOR. http://www.jstor.org (accessed 26 May 2014).

Literature Online. http://literature.proquest.com (accessed 26 May 2014).

Part Three
Creative Writing

CREATIVE WRITING: YEAR ONE
Sarah Dobbs

Introduction

This chapter tells you what to expect from your creative writing degree. I talk about the various ways you can study creative writing, what to do before you begin and what to expect from the teaching. I discuss assignments and consider extracts from student work and why they achieved the mark they did. There is also some consideration about what you can expect from Year Two. All of this is punctuated with advice from students past and present.

Beginning Creative Writing: What to Expect

God I'm envious of you. I've wanted to be a writer since *forever* – you might feel the same. I went to a couple of classes at my local college, but other than that I didn't know any other writers. I certainly didn't have the foggiest how you went about becoming one. Google didn't exist, so no answers there. All I had (I know, poor me) were my books, my imagination and a compulsion to write and record. You'll probably know what I mean – that *itch*, and no antihistamine will ever cure you of it. So I just wrote and dreamed, which probably feels like a similar story to you.

Fortunately, things have changed. I studied English literature at uni, mainly due to the fact that books were involved. Plus I'd been lured by the promise of being able to take a single creative writing module in the second year. These were 'first come, first served' and somehow I missed out. But hang on a sec while I step out of my time machine and get back to the present. So what's going on now? With the rise of creative writing degrees and the advent of the creative writing A-level, yours is a subject that is becoming rapidly more accessible, available and varied. It used to be that your first year (Level 4) was a basic introduction to the craft. At Level 4, amongst other things, you will learn how to generate new writing, to comment and critique other students' work, the importance of redrafting and basic strategies for how to plot and create characters. In the future, given that there will be students coming through with experience of creative writing at A-level, the shape of the degree is likely to change. Those writing and updating degree programmes will be taking into account the fact that an increased amount of first-year students would now have prior experience of creative writing.

But what can you expect of this experience? Below is part of the subject definition for NAWE's (National Association of Writers in Education) *Creative Writing Subject Benchmark Statement*. An increasing number of, but not all, universities use the principles and aims of this benchmark to design creative writing degree programmes. Given that it was only written in 2008 you can imagine how, in contrast to a more established subject like English, creative writing degree programmes are relatively new and developing all the time.

> Creative Writing is the study of writing (including poetry, fiction, drama and creative non-fiction) and its contexts through creative production and reflection on process. (May 2008, 12)

Hopefully, you can see from this the importance placed on both creating and deconstructing/analysing your work.

I'd been writing lots of fantasy fiction when I was younger. I loved getting lost in other worlds. For me, when I started studying the techniques of writing at university, and was opened up to a range of authors and genres that I didn't usually read, the way I wanted to write changed too. You might go in wanting to be the next Stephanie Meyer or J. K. Rowling, but find yourself compelled to experiment with a variety of other genres and types of writing. Embrace it. The first year especially is the time to experiment. Push yourself. Be surprised at what you can do.

Some students will seem to 'take' to their degree with ease. These will be the students whose work everybody seems to like. You'll hear comments like:

'Amazing.'

'This could be published.'

'I wish I could …'

And so on. Don't be daunted. It's not entirely true that people have a 'natural' talent for writing. They might have a natural talent for observation. They might have had experiences in life that make them thoughtful or intuitive regarding other peoples' emotions that translates easily to their writing. All these are skills that you can learn by reading and analysing other writing.

However, even these students will be undergoing some sort of battle to improve their work. They'll want to be the next big (fill in the blank) sooner than their talent will allow. And by talent, I mean 'talent'. In nearly all cases, good writing is actually just hard graft and thoughtfulness.

Creative writing *is* hard. So it's worthwhile knowing what to expect before you start your first year. This guide is here to help you as you progress through your degree, with helpful sound bites from previous students, tips from tutors and examples of mark schemes. There will be examples of student writing to demonstrate how and why certain types of work might gain a 1st, a 2:1 or even fail.

There are some brilliant craft books on creative writing. So our main aim is not to teach you how to write. It's to help you understand what's expected of you as a creative writing student and how best you can help yourself to study it. The book aims to equip you, as much as possible, to get through that process. You might also be considering whether a degree in creative writing is for you, or whether you would be best on a full or joint honours. We'll talk about that too.

What Types of Creative Writing Degrees Are There?

I thought I'd be able to focus on script, but we only ever did a few classes on it, the tutor was a novelist.

(Jennifer, Year One, BA Creative Writing)

Creative writing is often studied as part of another degree programme. Recently, more universities like Edge Hill, where I've worked, have started to offer complete programmes in creative writing. If you did a course like this, it's possible to only study creative writing. When you study creative writing as part of another degree programme, this could be as a joint honours or a major/minor option. With joint honours, you will study creative writing alongside another degree. The balance will be split 50/50. For example, half of your programme of study could be English and half creative writing. If you study creative writing as a major option, this generally means that around 75 per cent of your studies will be focused on creative writing, with the remaining part made up by modules from your minor programme. The reverse is true if you're studying creative writing as a minor option. This pattern generally continues throughout your whole programme of study.

In some universities, depending on your course, it's possible to take creative writing as an elective or a 'one-off' module. This means you might be able to undertake just one module in creative writing, no matter what programme of study you are on. It is important to consider when this would be a good idea. I once took an elective in beginners' Italian in my final year of an English degree. I did it because I knew I was fairly good at languages and thought it would boost my final degree mark. It could be a tricky decision to undertake a creative writing elective in your third year, if you have no prior experience and are aiming for a particular grade.

Another alternative is studying creative writing as part of an open degree via a distance learning institution. The way you're taught and how you'll learn is quite different than on a traditional, campus-based degree programme. At a 'bricks and mortar' university, you'll have face-to-face time with your tutors and fellow students. Some people thrive in an environment like this. Distance-based learning puts a lot of onus onto you to pursue your own study and keep up to date with the workbook, assessments and tasks. In a campus-based institution, I feel I have the opportunity to teach in lectures, seminars, tutorials and with my feedback on assignments. As a tutor with the Open University, which offers distance courses, most of my teaching takes place in their often lengthier marking forms. There are at least a couple of e-tutorials through the year, two day schools, as well as the opportunity to put some points across in the online forums. Some students enjoy the freedom of not having to physically attend on a particular day. It's also their choice whether they want to, or have the time, to participate in forums. My advice here is that the more you engage with fellow students online, your tutor, the programme and the activities set around it, the more you'll develop your writing. On a distance course, it's crucial you can manage your own time. Most tutors will be part time and work on specific days in the week, so you'll have less opportunity to get in touch. Distance learning is a great option for those needing flexibility. Some recent distance learning students of mine have set up their own regular writing workshop to help them stay in touch. Why not set one up yourself, whatever type of course you're on? There's no such thing as too much feedback.

What Should I Expect from the First Year?

However you're studying, as mentioned, the first year is often the time to experiment. Most of the universities that I am aware of do not count first-year grades towards your final mark. This is to help make sure everyone is on the same page (writing pun – I know, terrible, I should go on a course) and that you've found your footing. Adjusting to university life can be a bit of a job in itself. *This doesn't mean that you shouldn't work hard – you still have to pass!* Every year of your degree is important, but the first year gives a foundation for you to build upon. If studying modules as part of a distance learning degree, then your marks will absolutely count towards your final degree. You can still experiment as the percentages will be relatively low once all your other modules and years are taken into account. It's perhaps something to consider when deciding how you want to study, if you haven't chosen your degree already.

In the first year, you'll get an introduction to the various forms of creative writing. The most common are **Fiction**, **Life Writing**, **Script** and **Poetry**.

Fiction more often than not involves the study of short stories, micro- or flash fiction. Longer fiction, which could be longer stories, novellas, novelettes or the novel, is unlikely to be studied in the first year. You could also study script, which might involve radio, stage, film and TV. In some universities, script isn't encouraged. In some, it's studied throughout the whole degree. Similarly, some universities might not study the various genres separately. This might mean you don't really get the opportunity to fully focus on specific genres. Poetry and life writing will also be studied, at least in some form. Life writing, put simply, is the creative biography (even when focusing on specific events as opposed to an entire life) or autobiography. I'm not mentioning the variations in courses to worry you, but to help you choose the right degree programme if you haven't already. Don't just assume you'll get to study everything you want to. There is so much variety that you will certainly be able to find a course that provides the right balance for you.

What Will I Get Out of a Creative Writing Degree?

That depends on you. Right? Obvious, but true. How much work will you put into your study and development? Back to our first question: what will you get out of your degree? Study in creative writing inevitably leads to you being a better writer. This isn't as simple as it might sound. You might have the inclination to write – the itch, as I mentioned earlier – and be okay at it, but you could always be better. Follow one of those recipes for spag bol in that *Surviving Studentsville* book your mum bought you and you'll produce something edible first time round. As you get practised in making it, you might tweak the ingredients. Extra cheese is good. I like Parmesan and fresh basil.

(Note: extra cheese is not good in writing.) The point is, the more writing and rewriting you do, the better you're likely to get. Basically, what works is work.

True or False: Writers Are Born, Not Made.

There aren't often totally 'wrong' answers in a subject like English or creative writing, but if you think the above statement is true – well, you're wrong. Wrong wrong wrong! Writers are always working and reading and developing.

> I thought that you just wrote and I never bothered with drafts because I honestly thought what I wrote was amazing. I learned my lesson in the second year.
>
> (Mark, Year One, BA English and Creative Writing)

Be honest, do you agree with Mark? Once upon a time (sorry) – and this makes me cringe – I did. I loved writing and reading and getting lost in it. I thought I had something important to say. What did those students know – critiquing my work for being 'rough'? Turns out, a lot. My advice? Don't fall into this trap. There's *always* an extra draft. It will always make your work better. Apparently, Picasso was known for taking a brush to his paintings while they were in the gallery. Be Picasso. Meaning: be passionate enough to perfect your work.

So we know that creative writing can make us better writers, but what else will it do for you? You'll be encouraged to read as a writer. This means becoming self-conscious about your own work and others' work. That kind of focused analysis can lead to clear and independent thinking. You'll become your own critic, able to critique your own work and see the flaws in it. This skill and way of thinking is transferable – something employers could appreciate. Analysing flaws in plot structure or creative work might lead to a more considered structure in your essays. I once had a history student who thought his essay writing was boring. He wanted some creative skills to help make his essays more readable. Happily, both courses complemented each other.

What Should I Do before I Start?

You'll get a reading list before you start so get your hands on that as soon as possible and start reading. If you have spare time in the summer before you begin your course, read widely. Pick books you'd never read. Have a 'read-off'. By that I mean …

Task – Choose a book you dislike or wouldn't normally read for pleasure. It could be a classic – Dickens or Bronte. Now choose one you love. Focus on a particular element – the descriptions. Note how Dickens and your favourite author write. Why do you like one and not the other? Write a description of what's outside your window in each author's style. What have you learned by doing this?

Keep a notebook about your observations when going for a walk or scribble in it for at least half an hour a day. It doesn't particularly have to make sense. Most courses ask that you keep a writer's journal, so it's good to get into the habit of this. Some modules will even use the journal as part of the marking criteria.

Another good thing to do is to get one of the craft books mentioned in the bibliography and start working through those. Being familiar with terms and techniques might help with that settling-in process.

What Should I Expect from Teaching?

Often, the 'soft' courses don't have as much contact time as other programmes. If you think of science degrees, for example, you might be in the lab a lot doing things with Bunsen burners (do better research than me if you're writing about science students) as well as attending lectures, seminars and tutorials. On a creative writing degree, you'll likely have a combination of lectures, seminars or workshops and tutorials.

This is one *very basic* example for a week (your actual timetable might look quite different):

• four lectures at 2 hours each

• four seminars/workshops at 2 hours each

The rest of your week could be made up of non-timetabled study. While this might seem like free time and a great opportunity to get in a few extra shifts, it's really not. It's unstructured time for you to pursue the reading required for lectures and seminars, to commit to reading a lot of secondary material, such as craft books, novels, stories, scripts and, of course, writing and redrafting. If you're doing a *full-time* degree, the hours you're signing up to are *full time* too, not just the amount of hours you're in. This is why being organized is perhaps the best skill to learn.

Lectures

It is likely your lectures will coincide with what you discuss in seminars. They'll provide a theoretical grounding in a particular topic. Often giving an overview of a certain area, you might then be given secondary material/tasks to follow up on. For example, you might get an introductory lecture on endings in fiction, which uses examples from published work to demonstrate different ways of concluding a story, such as the **twist** or the **open ending**. In the workshop that week, you might then look at endings and play around with writing your own.

Seminars/workshops

In creative writing, seminars and workshops can be quite similar. In English, a seminar would be a much more detailed exploration of what is included in the lecture. It might include student discussion, analysis of critical responses to the texts you are looking at, as well as sample essay questions.

Workshops, however, are more often found on creative writing courses. Your lecturer or tutor will most likely respond to the lecture you've had for that particular module. They might take one aspect of the lecture and focus on it in detail. There'll always be a syllabus and a timetable, so you can see what you have to read or write from week to week. Some courses have much more structured reading than others and it's definitely worth taking the time to find the one closest to what you're looking for.

Workshops are also an opportunity to do some focused writing. Instead of reinventing the vampire myth (I was convinced I could do this – I couldn't), which you might play around with at home, your tutor might set exercises that highlight the theme of the lecture. What you've written in the workshop might be discussed in the session or finished off in your own time. Try to ensure you do these tasks and keep hold of them, redrafting when possible. It's likely you'll be able to include this work in a future assessment, one which will want to examine work created and reflected upon during the course. At other times, you'll be asked to bring in copies so you can discuss your work in detail. Above all, you should experience a variety of teaching methods. If there are elements you're dissatisfied with or want more of, then you'll have the opportunity to mention that in a review. Some things students have asked for in the past include more handouts, more focus on terminology, more time to write.

What Skills Will I Need to Demonstrate in the First Year?

In the first year, your tutors will be looking for you to meet first-year criteria. This criteria will increase and develop as you continue into Years Two and Three. Don't expect what's expected of you, or your marks, to stay exactly the same! Initially, we want to see that you have the ability to generate new work, that the work is written well and is interesting, there's a good use of description, intriguing characters and workable dialogue. But how can you do all of this?

Ability to generate new ideas

You will be given prompts and exercises that help you think of what to write. You can also get ideas from craft books. Even if you aren't writing full stories at this point, you want to aim for originality. Don't give us a Stephen King–type horror set in Maine. He's written loads of them – some are great. So what's the point? What about a horror set in the last corner shop in Ashton? Consider how the tone of the setting might enhance your writing and lend it something original.

Observation

What's the difference between saying 'it was hot' and 'the sun prickled his scalp'? One *tells* us information, the other *demonstrates* it. Only in the second example might you imagine your own scalp prickling and experiencing the sensation of heat. Use your journal to note how things really look and really feel. Use all the five senses.

Drafting

Repeat after me: Drafting is the key. Drafting is the key. If you leave yourself time to do even one redraft of your work, you might be ahead of the curve when you first arrive. If you write ten drafts … you get the picture. With each new draft, you'll get your work as mistake free as possible. But that's not the whole point. You want to ensure each word suits your purpose.

Task – Which one of these descriptions is more effective and why?

The water looked oily, viscous. Rain hammered its iron surface.

It was a dull day.

Critique

Who cares what people think of your work? You should. Sometimes, the hardest things to hear can be the ones that make the most sense. Those little flaws you'd been hoping people wouldn't notice. You should also prepare yourself for the fact that it takes people time to get good at critiquing.

These are some fairly common examples that I've heard over the years. Not exactly helpful, are they?

'I don't read this sort of stuff so there's no point.'

'Don't like it, don't know why.'

'It's all right, I suppose.'

'It's amazing! Nothing needs to change! Just more of the same!'

What's wrong with this? These students might be telling the truth. Well, it's far too vague to start with. You don't read this sort of genre? So what? You can't avoid commenting on Shakespeare in an English class just because there are no car chases in it. Imagine telling a physics lecturer that you'd quite like to forget about the Big Bang because it was ages ago? Tough. Whatever is in front of you, analyse it for its successes and ways it can be improved. You're not 'wasting time' on other peoples' work. Most likely, you'll realize what could be changed in yours too.

> Some people are constructive and some use it to try and make themselves look better, curry favour or have a dig.
>
> (Emily, Year One, BA Creative Writing)

A critique session will involve working with your tutor and each other as a group. All of you will comment on the work. These sessions can feel sluggish if people don't contribute. If it's not going well, try asking questions – if you could change anything, what would it be? I felt the dialogue wasn't realistic – the accent threw me. What did you all think?

Peer critique

Peer critique is a similar process to a general critique. The difference with peer critique being that the tutor *facilitates* the session, as opposed to being closely involved in giving feedback. This puts the onus on your fellow students to provide responses about your work. Often, you'll be expected to incorporate these responses into your reflective statements or commentaries. More on those later.

The rubric

This just means following the rules for an assignment. If you have to submit 750 words and you go over or under this by 10 per cent you can lose up to 10 marks in some universities. That's a serious waste of your hard work. Read the guidelines and make sure you follow them.

Assessment

Your assignments will most likely be formed from a variety of the following:

Portfolio

A collection of work that demonstrates your best writing. It isn't possible to give an example of a real portfolio here due to space. However, the way to get the best marks is always to pay attention to the assessment brief. A good rule of thumb is that you want to show diversity, but not at the expense of marks. If you're rubbish at dialogue but brilliant at description, either get brilliant at dialogue too, or put in a decent sample that's been critiqued a few times to help you, or play to your strengths. You want your selection of work to all be of a similar quality. Otherwise, a piece that's not as good could drag down your overall mark. Ensure all your selections are new work and not just stuff that's been rehashed from college. Your tutor can usually tell and wants to see how the course you're on right now is enabling the evolution of your writing.

Journal

At the beginning of your degree, you might be asked to keep an ongoing journal. This might be formative (not assessed) and just for your own thoughts and observations. If it's summative (assessed) the journal might need submitting for a percentage of an assignment's mark, or it might form an assignment of its own. Here, your tutor will be looking for progression, connection to the course, how and why your writing is changing. As always, check the rubric.

Author analysis

This could also be called reading as a writer, or something similar. It will take the form of an essay, not creative writing, and is basically the analysis of another author's work. This type of assignment is not about delivering a nice review of the author you're reading or to delve into psychological reasons for why the author is writing about Africa, for example. It's to talk about how they've achieved tense dialogue or sensual descriptions and how and why you have engaged with the characters. Give examples from the text, use craft books and critics' thoughts on terminology to support your discussion and explain how the author has constructed their work.

Commentary

This is like author analysis, but for your own work. Did you try to create a fully rounded character? Why did you choose this type of ending? What do you still need to work on? As above, use quotations from your own work and any other writer / craft text that might support what you're saying. Reference correctly.

Other types of assessments

As you progress through your degree, you'll encounter a variety of assessments, depending on your university and mode of study. You might be required to keep a **learning log** or **journal**. This could detail the project/writing you're working on, the research you have been doing and so on, your thoughts about your writing in general. The log/journal could be **formative** or **summative**. Formative assessment monitors learning but doesn't provide a mark, as summative does. It may be compulsory, though, so make sure you check. Other forms of formative assessment could include presentations (group or individual). For example, research a market to submit your work to. Though it's often a welcome change of pace for students to take charge of the class, the reasons for presentations are various. We want to equip you with the skills to work independently and in a group. We're also encouraging you to look beyond your degree – how will you get your work read? How should you approach an editor?

Creative assignments

I've left this one till last as it's the assignment that will most likely form the largest part of your assessment. That's only fair – it's a creative writing degree and it's probably what you're most looking forward to. For each module you do – whether that's fiction, poetry, script or life writing, you'll be assessed on how well you can demonstrate that particular type of writing. Again, you need to follow the rubric. What is this assignment looking for? Generally, your tutor will be looking for the same things that you would focus on in an author analysis. For example, you might have loved an author's use of description. Similarly, your tutor will be looking for original and lively description in your work, amongst other things. If you're writing a short story, then a good shape to this story, consideration for the beginning and ending and a sense of pay-off will be beneficial. You'll also be marked on how well you fit the form. Writing script might be very new to you. If you follow expected formatting – for example, how to present your cast list and stage directions – you'll be giving yourself a better chance of good marks. But fitting a form also means whether you've used that medium well. Have you just written rhyming couplets for poetry (this might show lack of consideration for the form)? Have you used sound to your advantage within a radio play? Or have you forgotten to use it at all? Think about the benefits of each medium and really try to utilize them for your writing.

How Can I Try and Get the Best Marks?

It's useful to try and understand the mark scheme for your particular course. Don't yawn – it's interesting! Okay, it's not, but being aware of the mark scheme can help you understand just what your tutors are looking for. Your tutors will all follow the same mark scheme. It makes sense to familiarize yourself with it.

> I think there are pretty good guidelines in place [for marking]. Of course, creative writing is so subjective.
>
> (Andrew, Year Three, Creative Writing module).

> I would have liked to understand the mark scheme better. I understood it better for English.
>
> (Paul, Year Three, BA English and Creative Writing)

Mark schemes and variations

Most universities work on the percentage scale. Your work is given a number out of 100, which results in a certain percentage – say, 71 per cent. Lucky you! Anything over 70 means you get a 1st, which is the top grade you can achieve. Some courses might grade you A–E and still others might define work on an excellent to fail structure. Familiarize yourself with your own institutions' grade boundaries. Below is an example of mark schemes that I have seen within creative writing.

Basic mark scheme:

All universities will have their own mark schemes that define what grade you will get for each piece of work. I have designed an abbreviated example of a mark scheme below. Be sure to pay close attention to your own university's mark scheme – it will likely be longer and more in-depth than the one provided here. However your own university's mark scheme is structured, an awareness of the scheme will enable you to place where you currently are in your work and where you would like to be.

70+ (1st): Work will be of a publishable standard and free from any errors. The writing will show flair, imagination and poise. Research will be thorough. Character, language and voice will be exemplary, sustained and appropriate to the genre and form.

60–69 (2:1): Writing in this band may offer potential for publication or performance. It will be edited to a very good standard. There will be some element of originality. A good level of research is to be expected. Achievement will be sustained, but may falter.

50–59 (2:2): Work will be competent and demonstrate an awareness of skills taught on the module. Further research might be required to develop the idea. There may be implausible or unrealistic elements. There may be some originality but writing and/or ideas might seem stale. Awareness of genre might be inconsistent.

40–49 (3rd): Some evidence of learning and technique might be apparent. May lack structure and originality. Presentation will be incorrect in some instances. Research will be required to strengthen underdeveloped ideas.

Below 40 (fail): May not use any of the suggested techniques and the idea will be unoriginal and in need of development. May not have adhered to the rubric of the assignment. Presentation will be very poor.

If you're trying to connect this mark scheme to one you understand better and if you've come to university via college, then a 1st would be an A, a 2:1 a B, and so on. For the mark schemes that use excellent to fail grade boundaries, a 1st would be an excellent.

Here is an example of a more complex mark scheme from Dr Cath Nichols, author of our final chapter and tutor at Leeds. You can see how it's useful to read the descriptions below the grades – this will help you check whether your work matches up to these, how you're likely to score and what you might need to do in order to improve.

75+: outstanding grade / high 1st (every aspect excellent but also original)

70–74: excellent grade / 1st

65–69: very very good (or a combination of very good and excellent) grade: a high 2:1

60–64: very good (or a combination of goods and very goods) grade: a 2:1

55–59: good grade: a high 2:2

50–54: fair to good grade: a 2:2

45-49: weak (possibly with one fair, but overall weak) grade: a 3rd

40-44: very weak (not enough work and/or some work is poor) grade: a weak 3rd

39 or below: fail (not only is there too little work, the work provided is *also* very poor)

Examples of marking in creative writing

Below are examples of two short extracts from student assignments, one that has scored highly and one that scored fairly low.

Extract from a portfolio piece (low scoring)

> I woke up and turned off the alarm. A new day, I think to myself. I brought my hand to my head and rubbed the sleep out of my hair. Suddenly, I jumped. Someone was in the room with me! He regarded me coolly. The most beautiful man I'd ever seen. But was he really a man? There was something ghostly in his cheeks. Something hungry. I was powerless to resist.

Why does this get a low score? It's cliché and implausible, not to mention a little too close to *Fifty Shades*. We see quite a few stories beginning with characters waking up and ending with them going to sleep. It's too familiar. Even car chases, if they're overly formulaic, can be dull. Imagine if there was some way you could ride a rollercoaster to work/uni everyday – you'd end up getting adjusted to it. Now, if someone you loved was on that rollercoaster and in jeopardy, the journey might be more exciting. Write out of your comfort zone, push yourself. I read a story recently about a woman who buys a handbag. That's it. She goes to a shop and buys a handbag. The End. Now, if the woman was middle aged, depressed or set in her ways and the last time she'd treated herself and bought a handbag was when she felt young and optimistic, then we have something closer to a story. Give the reader a reason to care about your work and the people in it.

How could we improve it? Let's try to adapt the portfolio piece.

'Emma.'

I closed my eyes, the lids felt swollen through tiredness. My throat was tight. Another night of not sleeping, because you were always there. 'Michael.'

It wasn't you. Okay, yes, I knew that. But I pretended you could hear me. That there hadn't been that day where, on top of everything, I'd had to flick through sale dresses last minute at the local Sainsbury's. Where I buried you, feeling like I was half-crouching, half-standing in a black wrap-over that was reduced from £25 to £6. My mother had been delighted – at the bargain. She'd liked you.

'Michael.'

I moved my lips, to kiss you. When we'd met, I'd done that too. Imagined what it would be like to kiss you. Would it be testing and clumsy? Back then, the fantasy had been vivid. I had all your cues to go off. Tonight, I moved my mouth in the air and tasted nothing.

Why would this be a higher-scoring piece?

While far from perfect, it gives us a stronger sense of character, for one. That's done by providing some hints about the backstory. We know about Emma's mother, how hard the funeral must have been. There's the sense that she thinks her grief is misunderstood or that people don't care (her mother was excited about the bargain of the dress). There are specifics – naming things like Sainsbury's or mentioning the exact prices add reality. The grief is contrasted with the delight of their first meeting and how she used to imagine kissing Michael, even though she can't any longer. It addresses her lost love as 'you', which is a little unusual and adds to the nostalgic tone. Writing like this would score a decent 2:1. To make it a 1st, we'd need something a little more original, perhaps in the descriptions themselves or the setting, more considered characters. But you can see how we have changed the original piece into work that utilizes more techniques and should have more of an impact on the reader.

Let's look at a high-scoring piece of work.

Extract from a portfolio piece (high scoring)

'None of your business.'

The woman on the bee-orange bus seat next to me says, 'Excuse me?'

'I said, none of your business.'

She frowns and her skin wrinkles like a drying peach. 'But I didn't ask you anything.'

There's a baby being jiggled on the opposite side of the carriage by a girl with heavy eyes, wet hair and a *yeah, and* expression. It's like she's shaking it down for spare change. I can't help but think, why her? Why her and not me?

Why does this get a high score?

Well it's not perfect, but it does at least try to be original with the descriptions – 'bee-orange'. It opens *in medias res* – you're already in the action. Something is happening now. There is tension – why is the first speaker causing trouble? Why isn't it fair that the young girl has a baby and the protagonist doesn't? What could have happened? All of these things ask questions and questions make a reader keep reading. This student has thought much more about how to construct their work and the impact all these little details might have on the reader.

Task – It might seem counterintuitive, but try and make this piece low scoring. Choose a grade boundary – say, 3rd. We don't want you to learn how to write poorly, but it can be useful to figure out what makes a piece of writing not work very well.

Extract from example analysis (low scoring)

I like this collection of stories. I think the cover is really nice and really grabs your attention. If I was in a shop I would buy it. One of the stories is about a university student, which I could identify with, but it also had different characters. Like the postman and the wife. These helped me see a broader spectrum of life.

Why does this get a low score?

It's not paying attention to the rubric. The assignment doesn't ask for a book review or comments on the cover design. It does start to talk about the text and if it goes on to discuss how these characters are created it might avoid failing.

Extract from example analysis (high scoring)

Alison Macleod uses two time periods in 'Dirty Weekend'. In France, her partner is vibrant but distant. In Brighton, he is dying but they appear close.

I can see how I could have adapted this technique for my own story 'Liminal', using a more pronounced period to show the development of my main characters' relationship.

Why does this get a high score?

This assignment scores highly because it gets straight into a discussion. The student analyses how the writer has used time in the narrative. Importantly, this is related back to the students' own work and how they feel they can improve. This is good because we want to see how analysing other writers helps you to develop your own writing. This is someone who is thinking about the impact and possibilities of technique. If the rest of the assignment has correct references and quotations from the text, as well as demonstrates evidence of reading from the course materials and secondary reading, it would be a solid mark.

A Note on Bibliographies

Some courses will simply want a list of books that have been used in your commentary or that helped inform the writing of that particular piece. Again, you need to check the purpose of this for each specific assignment.

As a rule, a sprinkling of texts in your bibliography isn't enough. You want to include books that are on your reading list, as well as appropriate secondary reading. It might seem confusing to try and add to your bibliography. What if you haven't read more books? That's one of the points the bibliography is there to make and measure. You need to be reading more. It'll help you write and help you write about writing. So depending on your assignment, you could include craft books or short stories / novels / scripts that have influenced the creative piece. You can also include readings you attended. Your department might have visiting writers or performances where writers might offer valuable information. (One recently said, cut all words ending in 'ly'. I'd been saying this for a year, but once the visiting writer said it, for some reason it clicked.) Going over ten is possibly too much for the first year, though no tutor will ever penalize you for a long bibliography, unless it seems obviously made up and irrelevant to the task. Don't just include books for the sake of a long bibliography. This will be obvious, especially if you don't refer to them in your commentary/essay.

Some universities request annotated bibliographies. This involves a paragraph under each text demonstrating how and why it has informed your writing. For example:

Barker, Pat. 1998. *Another World*. London: Viking.

This novel is about memory and helped me with 'Liminal' as it was also about the importance of past events on the present. I realized

I could be more suggestive with references to the past, as Barker was, and feed them in slowly.

What If I'm Not 'Good' at It?

It is clear that there are guidelines; however it is also clear that different tutors interpret those in different ways. Some prefer one style of writing and some another. Whilst these preferences may not have a big impact, they are bound to have some influence.

(Adam, Year Three, BA English and Creative Writing)

A common complaint from students is that creative writing is subjective, so marking is erratic. Tutors are more amenable to work they 'like'. There will be work that tutors do like more than others. Think about it. Why do you choose the next Bukowski or Atkinson? You like the style/pace/descriptions of one over the other. While it's fine to make personal choices at home, at work your tutor will be adhering to strict marking criteria. So if one of your pieces doesn't score highly, try to see it as a way to work out how you can do this in future. Is the plot too sluggish? Are the characters a little flat, the dialogue clunky? Are there grammatical errors?

Task – Look at a recent piece of your own writing and try and place it in one of the grade boundaries mentioned earlier. You could do this again when you are about to submit your first assignment. Where would you place your piece of work? Is it really of publishable standard? Would you read it in a bookshop and pay £5.99 for it? Does it require development? Be honest!

What If I'm Just Too Busy?

I wish that someone would just cook the tea for me once in a while!

(Suzanne, Year Two, BA Creative Writing)

Life is hectic. Isn't it? Sometimes, I wish I could put it on pause while I catch up – maybe there's a story in that. But seriously, you've probably got family, work, social life and now your degree to contend with. You've got to eat at some point too. Degrees are difficult when you're doing them full time, let alone when you have lots of other commitments to juggle. I went back to do my degree a little later in life, and every time I was in work I wished I was home so I could study. There is definitely a building of tension and worry about work you *should* be doing when you are doing something else.

The reality is, you probably won't be able to read everything on the reading list. You'll need help and you'll need to be organized. If you're doing this full/part time, remind yourself that even though it's a good stint, it's temporary. You will have to push yourself and work hard, but it's not forever and will be worth the sacrifice when you're in a funny cap and unflattering graduation gown, smiling for the millionth time at some very proud loved ones. Or … when you get that first acceptance for your writing.

For now, a timetable is your best friend. Get a year planner that you can put on your door, or the inside of your wardrobe. As soon as you know your assignment deadlines, mark them in on your calendar, perhaps colour coded per module. You'll be able to see at a glance what's coming up and how long you have to get ready. This calmed me down – *a lot*. Deadlines can feel like gremlins, creeping up at you from all sides. A proper planner is your 'bright light' and will help you feel in charge and prepared. A whiteboard that you can update might also be handy. In addition to your year planner, you can have a week-by-week planner that's easily updated.

Even at such busy times, it's important to schedule time off. A day's, or even an hour's, relief from work is crucial. Do whatever helps you relax – as long as it doesn't have damaging consequences! I find rubbish TV is perfect – as long as there's nothing nearby that I can write on or with. You can't keep up a permanent level of 'full speed ahead'.

Tips

- Get a year planner.

- Make a weekly study and work planner.

- Give yourself a 'time buffer'. Plan to get things done *before* it's needed. Things often go wrong with technology / cars / getting into uni to drop off an assignment.

- Submit before the deadline.

- Ask people in advance who are willing to babysit / help you out for an hour or two.

- Read as much as possible throughout the year, and particularly if you have any time in summer.

What Should I Do Between Now and Year Two?

Read and write.

Going from Year One to Year Two

It feels more pressurized in the second year as the grades count to your final mark. It is also quite a big leap; however, I do feel that good foundations were laid in the first year.

(Jennifer, Year Three, BA English and Creative Writing)

The first year was a real eye-opener. It laid so much out for me that I hadn't even considered. Or drew attention to things that I had noticed before, but had no idea how to harness; like the use of the senses, for instance.

(John, Year Three, BA Creative Writing)

Read more. But not just to read, to analyse how it's done. Sometimes it's easy to think that you're feeling a certain way (while reading) just because of your imagination. You're not. The writer has driven you there, pointed out the landmarks, and then you've looked around. How they do that (showing rather than telling, for example) is what you really need to learn. The crafting of the words.

(Jeff, Year Three, BA Creative Writing)

CREATIVE WRITING: YEAR TWO
Sarah Dobbs

Introduction

This chapter helps you understand what it is like to go from Year One to Year Two and the type of changes you will need to be making. You'll see comments from students who have been there – and survived! – and offer advice to help you with the transition. I talk about module options and credits and look more closely at assessments, discussing why it is so important to stick to the rubric of assignments. We look at an extended extract of a first-class piece of work and discuss why it achieved that mark. Finally, we consider how you might manage your time and what to expect from Year Three.

What's the Difference between First and Second Year?

Admit it. We've been lovely to you in the first year. What about all those wonderful short story collections we 'suggested' you read and analyse for how the author constructs character? How nice of us was that? You're saying you didn't enjoy standing up and reading your work and then having the rest of the class get their teeth into it and shake? Or that time we thought it would be a great idea to pretend you were a tree and write for 30 minutes on the passage of time? No? Interesting … everybody else did. Joking aside, some of the ways of learning and sharing work might have seemed like unusual torture – I certainly didn't enjoy reading my work or being critical of other students' writing. Hopefully, we've helped you get a little more used to critiquing work and having work critiqued – it won't feel as painful, or personal, in the second year. Good.

So now you can get down to business. Crack your knuckles, sharpen those pencils, charge the iPad and get the coffee on. Time for Year Two.

> I'd have kept a writer's journal from the first year on. A notebook of what I was learning each week and book quotes and page numbers and stuff like that. I did start to do it in my third year, but I wished I'd started earlier.
>
> (Shazia, Year Two, BA Creative Writing)

> Keep notes in the workshops and treat the teaching a bit like a mini-lecture. It all makes sense at the time and you think it's going in – but then afterwards you forget what everyone was talking about!
>
> (Martin, Year Three, Creative Writing module)

> One of the main differences that I found was in the practical aspects of writing. That is, in the second year I was reading, analysing, studying and writing every day. It took the first year to get to this point. So the first year is a means to gain the momentum and understanding that the second year is built on.
>
> (Craig, Year Three, BA Creative Writing)

So is Year Two just more of the same, or do you need to be 'better'? Predictably, it's the latter. We want to see you develop and second-year marking will measure that development. A few students have said, 'But I got a 1st for prose in Year One!' It's best not to fall into that trap. As you progress, it's a given that you're continuing to learn and we want to see that put into practice. Put simply, we want to see your work getting better. You've got all that new reading/writing/redrafting/critiquing experience that's making you more conscious about the choices you make in your work. Show us all that in the work you submit. Years ago, when I was first studying art, I got extremely excited by ideas but forgot I was rubbish. I hadn't learned any techniques. My tutor would ask how I planned to construct these ideas. I'll just paint, I said. Why paint? he said. Why not charcoal? It's a lesson I'll always remember. He was asking why I'd made my choice; I hadn't. I hope you're frothing with ideas. I also hope you're still reading and analysing other people's work to see their technique. How've they done that? Nick it. Try it. Emulate it. Draw a picture of a story. Whatever helps you understand how something has been put together. Again, look at your craft books and attempt their exercises to help you extend your writing and experiment with technique. There are a few examples overleaf to help you see just how easily writing can be changed. What you don't want is for your writing to always be static and sound like you. By pushing your natural style with tasks like these, you'll learn how a writer can affect a reader and how important technique is to this process. Perhaps most importantly, make choices, ask questions. Why paint, not charcoal? Why third person limited, not omniscient?

Task –

1. **Choose a section – a paragraph is fine – of any published book or story that is descriptive, perhaps of the landscape or a person. Think of your campus or home and describe it using the author's style, right down to their sentence structure.**

2. **Play with your writing by altering small details like the ones below. Do this with your campus/home description – you can also try it with the published work. Make the writing sound formal/informal, old/young, highly detailed / sparse, negative/optimistic. You can repeat this as many times as you like and with your own ideas.**

3. **Choose a tone – wistful, yearning, rejected, fearful, joyous, pensive, etc. – and redraft some of your writing so it sounds and feels like this.**

I can understand if you feel a bit unnerved at suddenly needing to be 'better'. You'll be worried that marking will be harsher and that your grades might suffer. It's true that what's expected from you in Year Two will be different, but it's cumulative. Meaning, if you've been going to all the lectures, seminars and author visits and doing the writing, redrafting and reading, you should be ready for Year Two. You'll have absorbed all the lessons and techniques from Year One and will be looking to start honing your writing. If you're reading this before you even start your degree (which is brilliant) remind yourself to attend and *do* all the exercises. Although there is a lot of theory around creative writing, the learning is in the doing.

Task – Compare the writing you've just done for the previous task with early first-year work. In what ways do you think your writing has improved? Are your descriptions more realistic? Are you making more deliberate choices in this writing? (Does your brain hurt? Always a good sign!) Could you have done this task as successfully in the first year?

How Is the Marking Different?

We've talked about marking and grades in Year One. What you need to know for Year Two is that the descriptors for those grades can alter across the levels.

The same is true of Year Three. If you look in a module handbook for Year Two, you should find a mark scheme. To get a 1st or a 70, it might say that your 'work should be of near-publishable standard'. The same isn't true of your work in the first year. That would be a big ask.

At Year Two, you should be producing work of near-publishable standard for a grade of 70 plus. We know now that you've got a year of experience under your belt. Late nights and redrafts of searching for the right verb. If there was any allowance for errors in the first year, whether that's in the proofreading or flaws in the work itself, it's likely there'll be less to none in the second year.

Sometimes, in Year Three, the learning outcomes for a 70 or above will change to 'publishable standard'. What does this mean? That you definitely have to get this piece of work published? That's not a requirement, but it does mean that the piece should be suitable for publication.

If you think about it, what does that mean?

- There should be no errors.
- It should be technically excellent.
- It should be an interesting read and engage its audience.

These three requirements can be broken down even further. Technically excellent, for example, means a story that opens well, ends well and has a good internal structure. If a story doesn't end well, and this doesn't mean happily, then it won't meet this criteria and it's unlikely it will be an excellent. These are things to keep in mind for Year Three.

What Will You Study in Year Two?

This depends on your pattern and programme of study, but you'll probably start to specialize. This could be a happy thing for many of you – maybe you were traumatized by the poetry modules, or struggled with script. Keep in mind when choosing modules that each medium has things to teach you. How concise are the descriptions in poetry, for example? How dynamic is the dialogue in script? Generally, all creative writing students will get a grounding in fiction and poetry and some courses do also allow you to study life writing and scriptwriting.

In your second year, you'll be able to choose options. If you're a full-honours student, you'll have more choice. In some cases, you might have a **core module** – one that everybody needs to study. This could be the creative writing workshop. A workshop like this often allows all creative writing students to work together, no matter what their specialist subject. As mentioned above, it can be really useful to work with writers of other genres because it allows you to appreciate and transfer the elements that are good about them. For example, life writing can transform a seemingly mundane event into an engaging piece of work. How? The creativeness with which its expressed? Many prose writers could benefit from this. I once read a piece of life writing about drowning that began, 'Pop-pop! Gurgle! Plunk!' It used sound to describe the sense of going under water in a fast-paced, frenetic way, instead of telling us what was happening (e.g., 'The man was going underwater'). Interesting **choice**, right?

Getting back to the basics of your year – it will most likely be broken up like this:

Full honours

Semester A

- core module (20 credits)

- option (20 credits)

- option (20 credits)

Semester B

- core module (20 credits)

- option (20 credits)

- option (20 credits)

120 credits – all made up of creative writing modules

Joint honours

Semester A

- creative writing core module (20 credits)

- creative writing option (20 credits)

- joint honours option (20 credits)

Semester B

- joint honours core module (20 credits)
- creative writing option (20 credits)
- joint honours option (20 credits)

120 credits – made up of 60 credits from creative writing modules and 60 credits from your joint honours subject.

Obviously, as mentioned in Year One, some of you reading this book might not be at campus-based universities. You could be distance learning students, doing one or two creative writing modules as part of an open degree. The pattern of study could be quite flexible here – one module per year. This means that you may not have modules to choose, or not have the same pressure to focus on a particular medium. I also teach with the Open University, and their Level 5 and 6 modules both require you to explore and attempt a variety of mediums. You can't, say, just do fiction the whole way through. This is something to keep in mind if you're thinking of doing a course or module like this.

On a typical degree programme, however, the options available will allow you to start pursuing the path or paths that most interest you. For example, you might choose to study fiction and scriptwriting. Don't take your option choices lightly, because they'll often have major implications for Year Three. If, for example, you drop poetry at this level, it might not be possible to resume it next year. I've said it before, but creative writing is a cumulative discipline. What's that mean? Just that you are expected to develop, gain experience, and become better writers because of it. If you skipped a year's training in poetry (let's call it that) then you could feel disadvantaged, and might not be able to pick it up again in Year Three.

For some degrees, learning is not like this. It might not be necessary to study romanticism in Year Two in order to study modernism in Year Three, for example. It could certainly help, as it would enable you to see the progressive nature of literature, but the other modules you're doing would enhance your critical and reading skills to the point that you should still be able to do another literature module.

Creative writing is a different discipline in this respect. You will be progressing as a writer and the work you produce must demonstrate this. We need to see evidence of previous learning in your work and the fact that you've engaged with the course. This is a really important point to keep in mind. Engage with your degree for three years and you'll see the rewards.

This is what a previous student said, about how hard creative writing actually is (this is not meant to put you off!):

> Creative writing is a craft that requires awareness, focus, time and effort to learn and practice. The creative writer is also perhaps one of the most exposed and, in a sense, vulnerable of all the craftsmen, and it takes a lot of discipline to be able to be both vulnerable and confident at the same time. When taken seriously, creative writing demands a lot and rewards a lot – when taken seriously, creative writing is absolutely not a soft option.
>
> (Joe, Year Three, BA Creative Writing)

I couldn't have put it better.

What Will the Assessments Be Like in Year Two?

Let's look at one module in particular to try and make this clearer. Your own modules will differ, but it's a useful exercise. Think about how you can apply our example here to modules on your own degree.

Intermediate Fiction

Credits: 20

Length: One semester

Delivery: One 2-hour weekly lecture and one 2-hour weekly seminar

Assessment:

A) One 2,500-word short story (80 per cent) with reflection (20 per cent) and drafts (compulsory)

B) One 2,500-word critical analysis of set text (100 per cent)

Assessment split: 50/50

But what does it all mean?

Credits: The amount of credits you get for the successful completion of this module is 20. This will go towards a total of the whole year's study, which almost without exception is 120.

Length: It takes place over one semester.

Assessment A: There are two assessments. Assessment A is a short story and is worth 80 per cent of your mark for this assignment. You're also asked to write a reflection – this basically means analysing what you did well and what could be improved.

Assessment B: This is a critical assessment. It assesses your ability to read a piece of literature, most likely one that is on the reading list, and evaluate the techniques that the author has applied.

We're going to look at an assessment in detail in a moment, but I just wanted to mention the differences you might experience with modules and credits if studying on a distance learning degree. With the Open University, for example, the Level 5 module (A215 – Creative Writing) is worth 60 credits. You'll study this one module for a whole academic year, often on its own, but sometimes students choose to do it alongside another module from a different discipline, such as English, history or music. There are five assessments staggered throughout the 32 weeks. While there are only two face-to-face tutorials, there are still weekly tasks that can be submitted via the online forums or worked through in your journal. If studying for an open degree, for example, the 60 credits you'll gain if you pass this one module will count towards the 360 credits you need to pass your degree.

Let's look at an extract of a story from a Level 5 (Year Two) student from the intermediate fiction module shown earlier.

Task – Read through this extract and decide what mark you would give it before reading the explanation below.

Stained

Fourteen's hands are cracked and sore from the day's toil. Twelve hours in the station laundry with harsh chemicals make for warped knuckles and fragile skin prone to split at the slightest knock. It's back-breaking work, heaving the large trolleys to the vat and throwing the overalls in by hand. Avoiding the acid burns in the fabric takes a quick eye; especially when working at the speed required by the ever watchful Command.

It is the end of the shift and for Fourteen a change in the rota. She clocks out, carrying her hands like a surgeon prepped for a procedure. Her ID card is at her waist, she uses her hip to activate the doors and her elbows to protect her hands from getting bumped. They throb in time to her heartbeat. She catches sight of her reflection in the door porthole. Her split lip is healing but her bruised jaw is still tender and sore. She is joined by other female workers as they trudge to the canteen for the end-of-shift meal. She nods her greeting to her friends: Ten and Forty-Six. Head-scarfed and clad in overalls, the women are like a column of penguins marching to the sea.

Ten eyes Fourteen's hands with a wince and whispers, 'Where are you due tomorrow?'

'Sanitary duty,' she replies.

'No talking in the corridor,' crackles Command from a speaker overhead.

Forty-Six glances towards the camera and nudges Ten into silence.

The canteen is a large unit with two serving hatches, two seating areas and a thick red line down the middle. The light is harsh and makes the workers look jaundiced. A gantry runs across the middle and two armed droids monitor the segregated room.

She picks up a tray, gasping as her fingers protest at the fine motor skills she's asking them to perform. She drops the tray onto the rack and nudges it along with her elbow. Lumpy stew is ladled into plastic bowls and accompanied with hard crusty bread. Fourteen drags the tray to the edge of the ledge and tries to grasp it. Her grip fails once, she takes a breath and goes again. Pain shoots up her arms as carries her tray to the nearest available seat. She lets the tray drop the last inch, glaring at her hands, which have stiffened into arthritic claws.

Ten and Forty-Six join her. They make an unlikely threesome. Ten is one of the youngest at the station, her face an uncensored riot of how she feels at any given time. Forty-Six is older, crows feet and a limp proclaim her seniority. She learnt a long time ago not to give much away.

'Are you okay?' asks Forty-Six.

'I will be after some sleep and food,' Fourteen replies.

'What about tomorrow's rota change? You can't do it with those hands, you'll pick something up,' Ten adds.

Fourteen shrugs, 'There's nothing I can do about it.'

A droid glides across the gantry and scans the women's half of the canteen; the three women fall silent. Ten starts describing her day in hydroponics and the droid goes back to its position.

They spend the rest of the meal talking about anything else, chewing hard at the stringy meat and assorted root vegetables. Ten and Forty-six clear the table so that Fourteen doesn't have to and she gives her friends an exhausted smile.

The doors at the far end open and the first of the men arrive for their post-shift meal. Ten glances across, scanning the faces, hoping to see her brother.

'No communication is permitted between Units A and E,' crackled the recorded message through tinny speakers.

Ten sighs heavily shaking her head. 'It's been four days.'

Fourteen's guts tighten. 'Look again tomorrow.'

Back at the bunk room Forty-Six searches her locker and retrieves a small tub. 'I thought I still had some left.'

'What?' asks Fourteen.

'Anti-bac barrier cream, I liberated some from medi-bay.' Forty-Six waves the tub at Fourteen. 'For your hands girl, come here.'

Fourteen does as she is told and holds her hand out. Her friend takes a small amount and gently spreads the goopy substance over her sore hands and wrists. It stings at first and then it begins to soothe and cool them.

'Thank you.' A knot of tension she has been carrying ebbs away.

'Re-apply before your shift starts, the protection gear in sanitation is a joke.'

'I know.' She glances upwards. 'Maybe I should have gone along with it.'

'Don't say it,' says Ten, her voice sharp.

'I'm beat. I've got to be alert tomorrow.'

(Jane, Level 5 Creative Writing Distance Learning degree)

What did you give it? You don't have to be right! It can be really hard to give a piece of work a definite grade, especially when you're not used to doing it and you haven't seen the ending. Don't worry if you're miles out. Looking at work like this and trying to grade it will help you consider where your own work might be placed. If you know that, you might also be able to think about what needs to change for you to gain higher marks. Writing isn't all about marks and success, it's so much more – it's a consideration of the world around us, an expression of ourselves, but for degree purposes, it's worth having all the facts.

Task – This assignment was given a 1st. Think about all the reasons that might put it in that excellent band – before you read the feedback below!

Extract from the feedback:

> 'Stained' is an accomplished genre piece with some dark undercurrents and felt well realized and realistic. I was interested straight away in Fourteen's situation and the harsh monotony of her and her friends' lives.
>
> I occasionally felt it was a little like *A Handmaid's Tale* (Atwood 1985), though the ending and theme alters this opinion somewhat. I did feel that there could have been a little more tension in the opening given what Fourteen was about to do. It's tricky given the word count, but I felt a little more detail/planning/obstacles could have heightened the sense of conflict.

You can see that there are still suggestions for improvement. This piece was a really engaging read and scored in the 70s, but responding to these comments before perhaps submitting to a short story market would be worthwhile. It's possible to get very high 1sts, or excellents – all the way up to 100.

Other Types of Level 5 Modules/Assessment

Some institutions will offer vocational modules at this level. This doesn't mean, as nice as that would be, holing up in a cottage and 'being a writer' for a few months. It means working on a project that has something to do with the professional world of writing. This could mean editing a journal, or producing an online magazine. Even though you're acting in an editorial capacity, your selections and arrangements of writers' work might shed valuable information on the importance of editing, which is really where the bulk of the work takes place.

There are many variations of projects and you will most likely be given a supervisor to help ensure you stay on track and have set measurable, useful and attainable goals. Owing to the variety of projects you could undertake, the assessment on these modules could also be varied. You might be asked to produce samples of the journal/magazine you have worked on, as well as a reflective essay which explores what you have learned. Some centres might arrange a viva, which is where you will be examined orally by a combination of experts and lecturers. This is still quite rare, but there's a lot of pressure on to vary assessment patterns and to ensure assessment is fair for all students.

What's the point of projects? We want to start preparing you for the world of work outside academia. Most writers earn a living via a combination of teaching, writing and other work. 'Other' could signal anything from working part time in a restaurant/shop/bank, to editing or bidding for project funding.

Some courses have an assessment where you are asked to single out a market. I mentioned this briefly in Year One, when discussing formative assessments and presentations. I teach one module which assesses this summatively (the mark counts towards your overall grade). For this assignment you have to find a market for a short story and produce a piece of work which meets that magazine's particular brief. This means you must stick to the word count and house style (the format, spelling and presentation that this market prefers). As with the presentations, assignments like these are ways of helping you prepare to be a writer outside the course. We've planned them for a reason, so try to see the merit in them and don't approach it as a box-ticking exercise. Maybe you could even submit that story after the course.

Other courses might ask you to look for a writing-related proposal and attempt to produce a professional and interesting brief that might very well be in with a chance of winning. You will probably not be required to submit the proposal for the job, only for your course. However, it means you'll have taken some steps to learn the business side of writing and be better prepared to find work at the end of your degree. We want to make you a better writer, yes. We also want you to create opportunities and practise skills such as proposal writing that might help you get funding for freelance or project-based work. There's something entrepreneurial about writers and you'll learn more about this as you progress to Year Three. In the past, I've managed to create jobs for myself by asking libraries if they'd like me to run a writing course, setting up a small business that runs non-academic writing courses and helping writers edit and structure their own work. Be prepared to keep an eye on how things are changing and find a niche that works for you. With libraries closing and people feeling nervous of rising fees, less students have opted to study creative writing as a hobby. That means my own courses, which have no qualification attached to them, have attracted more customers than previously. How might you be able to use the skills from your creative writing degree, not just to write, but to earn money that let's you continue writing?

Critical-Creative Projects

In addition to vocational projects, some institutions offer students the opportunity to choose an area of writing or writing theory that interests them and to develop a sustained critical or critical-creative piece on that. At Level 5, a project like this might be like a mini-dissertation and take place over one semester in place of regular face-to-face teaching. Again, you might have workshops and tutorials with a supervisor to track your progress. I did some external marking for one institution recently and read a wonderful piece on absence in fiction and how this could be constructed. The student analysed published writers for the varying ways that absence could be portrayed in a narrative and the impact of this on the reader, all supported with the appropriate terminology and critical comment. Another student considered the purpose of writing about grief, with an examination of published work and authorial technique – how authors presented grief. A creative response to this followed – a story which utilized varying techniques learned in the critical essay. For me, this demonstrates the importance of the conversation between the critical and the creative. If you can be logical about the analysis of creative work and use this analysis in your own writing, you'll become a better writer. In the third year and beyond, you might well start to use these skills to consider larger, more far-reaching and fascinating questions – why do we write being the most basic and perhaps most complex. But also questions like: What's the importance of recording grief creatively? Why not simply relate factual instances of grief? How might creative explorations of grief differ between cultures and what does that tell us about people? From here on in, you can start to see that creative writing as a subject has so many possibilities. Of course it's about great writing, lively details, original language and mesmerizing characters. It's also an exciting way of provoking and exploring all the big issues, questions and mysteries that surround us. But how do you become a good writer?

Building Your Skills from First to Second Year: The Overt Importance of Subtext

The purpose of a degree in creative writing is to develop intelligent students, not just intelligent writers. Subtext is likely going to be one of the differences between your work at Year One and Year Two. It is the difference between a piece of work that has consciousness and one that doesn't. So what does it mean when a piece has consciousness? It is, I suppose, the equivalent of 'reading between the lines'. A writer might indicate something that is not explicitly said in the text, and is hence not overt but implied. In other words, they leave space, or create an opportunity for the reader or the viewer to interpret, to be active. Every word they use does more than simply represent the image, but gives us a suggestion of how to respond to that image.

Task – What is the difference between this extract and the one below it?

1. Rubbish ringed the bin. She'd forgotten how much rubbish was in this city.

2. Crippled cans of Fosters ringed the bin, overlaid with decaying confetti.

What's the difference? The second is more specific. Specificity is good. Name things, know things. Why? It shows a writer who is clearly visualizing the scene they are creating. It shows authority. In addition to this, the verbs and nouns have strength – they *do* more and therefore demand our attention. They're interesting and this suggests we need to explore them. Why are the cans crippled and not just crushed or empty? Why has the writer chosen to juxtapose (put together for an effect) the confetti with the Fosters? Petals are quite pretty and reminiscent of nature, whereas cans are man made, harsh objects. Why are the petals decaying?

One reading is that the cans are crippled to reflect a sense of damage. This also fits with the description of the confetti petals. We would associate confetti with a happy occasion – getting married. But these petals are dying. Overall, the effect of just these two lines allows the writer to create quite a negative tone. This could fit, or contrast, with the rest of the piece. Whatever it does, it does more than the first two lines. These are straightforward and not particularly conscious.

Just one note here, this isn't an attempt to get everyone to write like this, but to demonstrate the thoughtfulness that has gone into the creation of these lines. And that's what we're looking for: evidence of thought. Why have you constructed something in a particular way, for what purpose and is it successful?

There is, of course, no guarantee a reader will follow your suggestions, but you are creating signposts. You're allowing for the possibility of an active reader, one who has more work to do and, perhaps, more connection to your writing.

Some Things to Remember

The following are some 'things to remember' that should help you write with intelligence and thought. Remember to read this book alongside a good craft book that will expand much more on technique and contain exercises like this.

- How could you express what you've written in as few words as possible?

- Does it begin *in medias res* (in the action)?

- Are the descriptions aesthetic (do they just look nice) or do they contribute to the story's overall meaning?

- Are you paying attention to the assessment brief? (If it's meant to be a story about Manchester and you've written about Victorian London, however brilliant it is that might be a problem.)

- Have you thought about the feelings the ending will create in the reader?

- Would your writing hook you? Would you buy it?

- What mark would you give your own work? (Be honest.)

What If It's All Going Wrong?

In my opinion, writing is like drawing. Or anything, for that matter, which requires hard work and an understanding of the skills that help make it good. Shred basil on that spag bol we were talking about in Year One and it tastes different, fresher. Similarly, attention to detail is one of the key elements that make good writers and by now, if you've engaged with your course and your tutors, you should have developed in this area.

If you're not doing well, ask yourself some difficult questions. Have you done all the required reading and followed up on your own interests? Have you actually been writing and rewriting? Have you zoned out in a critique session and given half-hearted responses? Marking is a rigorous process. For example, samples of all assessments are second marked. If you realize you haven't been engaging with the course as well as you should have been, then the solution is fairly simple: start now. Next year will be too late. But it's also useful to be honest with yourself. Why haven't you been doing the work? Are you too busy? Why? Are you working too much? Work is an absolute necessity for many students, especially nowadays, but you might need to try and make some adjustments. One of my students was failing. He'd considered his course to be part time because the programme leader had managed to schedule classes over two days. This was to help students who worked and had other commitments. We mentioned hours in Year One but it's important to reiterate – remind yourself that a full-time degree, even if you only have 10 contact hours, requires between 10 and 20 additional study/writing/learning hours. That leaves you with about 7 hours to do a part-time job and a very packed timetable.

What If You Really Don't Have Time to Put the Work in?

If your issue with time is work related, it might be possible to simply cut back. If you can't afford to reduce your hours, talk to your boss about having more flexible working arrangements. This could mean working at weekends, or changing your work patterns so they're more ad hoc. Many employers are quite sympathetic to students. On my degree, I worked in an office at the university and took on extra hours only if I was ahead with assignments. If you need the same amount of money, think about asking to work your hours over fewer days. Can you work from home? Quite a few businesses are more amenable to this these days. If you're forced to lose money, ensure you go to student services and ask about bursaries or hardship funds. It can take a while to apply, so think about your situation well in advance. For example, if you anticipate needing support for the next academic year, you need to start applying for it well before the end of the current academic year. Each institution will have different deadlines, so make sure you find out about them and don't miss out.

On the other hand, there are some people who might simply realize that writing isn't for them. Perhaps you'd thought it would be easy, or that you were naturally good at it or have found that you write better outside of academia. Maybe, if you're doing a joint honours, you're just doing far better in your other subject and want to focus on that so creative writing doesn't bring your marks down. Whatever your reason for wanting to change, you need to speak to your personal tutor as soon as possible.

One student I worked with recently was getting consistently low scores in the creative writing part of her degree, specifically poetry. She wanted to be a teacher, so it was important she got a good degree in order to compete for placements. No matter how much she attempted to respond to tutor feedback and to apply herself to the requirements of the assessments, she couldn't raise her grade. By contrast, she was happy with her marks in fiction, but they were at least a band above the ones for poetry. This was affecting her overall grade and looked like it would also lower her final mark. After speaking with her tutor, she was advised to drop the creative writing element of her degree. She still likes writing and had said that she would continue to write outside of the degree programme. This was the best option for her.

Basically, if you're having trouble, speak to someone as soon as possible.

How Should I Prepare for Year Three?

The best way to prepare is always to read, and to read thoughtfully. Authors can answer so many of our own questions in ways that textbooks simply can't. The irony, having a textbook tell you that! But it's true. When you can really see how someone else has constructed their work, it provides you with the knowledge to practice or the ability to think lucidly about your own structures. So again, keep reading over the summer. Analyse what you read. Write. And then write more. Get the reading lists as soon as possible, and try to read ahead. The fact that you need to *read* and *write* on a creative writing degree can be forgotten in first year. You've been having too much fun scaring yourself witless reading your work aloud. It's understandable. But read. Do it now. Read in the summer, on the bus, before bed, when you're supposed to be listening to your mum/partner/kids. Show them this book and tell them we told you it's okay to be absorbed in your own work for a while. It'll all pay off, eventually. Shlomith Rimmon-Kenan talks about the act of reading being intrinsically connected to time, that texts 'implicitly keep promising the reader the great prize of understanding – later' (1999, 124). It's a nice parallel then that the cumulative effect of all your reading and creative work should lead to good writing – later.

What Can You Expect from Year Three?

If the first year got me used to working consistently, then the second year built the layer of consideration and awareness of my work and other works. The third year built on this, and I was able to focus a lot more on philosophies, both of writing and within the works I create. I found I experimented a lot more, and a lot more successfully, sometimes obviously and sometimes beneath the surface of the piece. My thought, and then by extension my work, gained increased depth and awareness.

(Joe, Year Three, BA Creative Writing)

CREATIVE WRITING: YEAR THREE
Cath Nichols

Introduction

This chapter will offer a discussion of areas of the creative writing or joint degrees that have not been addressed in previous chapters. It will show you a sample of poetry from a student awarded a high 2:1 and then a rewrite of that to show how the *same content in a different style* would have been awarded a lower and a higher grade. There will then be some guidance on how to present your final portfolio. This chapter will also discuss the prospect of a work placement and what you should remember about your role within that placement. It will finish with a few suggestions of where to take your writing next: what questions to ask if you are considering an MA, and where to look for opportunities to share or publish your work.

Many courses arrange their teaching so that script and poetry modules come in the second or third year. At Level 6 (third year) the demands are higher. At Level 6 you are expected to:

- be fluent in using the concepts and theories related to writing as tools for investigating, analysing and developing your approach to writing creatively;

- engage with a wide range of complex and challenging sources including appropriate material that you have identified on your own initiative;

- undertake a sophisticated critical and creative approach – asking searching questions of both the work that you are developing and of your approach as a writer with reference to wider reading, refining an informed approach to writing creatively;

- have engaged fully with the creative process, exercising independence as a self-directed learner and writer – pursuing and refining your ideas to generate a carefully crafted piece of writing developed from your original, creative ideas; and

- communicate complex material in a clear, structured way that is appropriate for the assignment and observes industry conventions in formatting.

You will need to attend to your own university's more detailed criteria, which will be broken down for short story, novel, poetry, script and life writing. What this means in practice will become clearer with an example of a task and a piece of marked work.

Task – An example of 'strong word choices', which are extremely important to poetry, can be found in the following exercise. Look at this line: 'The apes stretch and _____ their fleas in the sun.' Think of three or four possible words to fill in the blank and jot them down now. We will come back to this.

It is difficult to quote from a poem to explain why the poem received a 1st or a 3rd, as a poem is valued for the way it binds together. Likewise with scripts. So bear that in mind as you write them: How 'whole' do they feel? Do they need every line? Every word? If you ditched a line here or there, or altered a word, would it matter? If it would not, then you may not have found the best shape for your poem. (This does not apply quite so precisely to poems beyond a page in length, but for the short lyric poem you must try to create something that feels welded into its final shape.)

Marked Example of a Poem

This is a poem from a student's submission of three poems in a final portfolio of work:

'Side Effects'

Awkward popcorn spilt on salty laps. The film

is unfinished, there's still time for some action. Knuckles rest on

thought out knees, every detail matters, cradling

the elephant in the room with damp palms. Side Effects

of the hummingbird patter within your chest.

Will he? Won't she? Should I? but would he?

Questions make the air tense. Forget it, focus on the film, but look

Intelligent, alluring, strong, sexy.

Don't gawp with your mouth open, you'll get a dry mouth,

Side Effects of a nervous date. A sneaky trip to the bathroom to pucker up

with some Vaseline won't poke the elephant. Don't poke the elephant. Let him.

The film's concluding and the lights expose our affected bodies:

Jittery, still, clammy, and dry. But then

A kiss to end an unromantic film.

As it stands the individual poem might gain a 67–8. It has moments of excellence but could be tightened up. Had it been written for Level 4 or 5 it would easily achieve a 1st. But for a 1st at Level 6 I would have made minor alterations: removed some of the capital letters; adjusted a few line-breaks; changed 'cradling' to 'We cradle'; removed 'sexy' ('alluring' is better and already present) … Spot the difference with this version:

'Side Effects' (2)

Awkward popcorn spilt on salty laps. The film is unfinished,

there's still time for some action. Knuckles rest

on thought-out knees, every detail matters.

We cradle the elephant in the room with damp palms.

Side effects of the hummingbird patter within your chest.

Will he? Won't she? Should I? Would he?

Questions make the air tense. Forget it, focus on the film,

try to look intelligent, alluring, strong.

Don't gawp with your mouth open, you'll get a dry mouth,

side effects of a nervous date. A sneaky trip to the bathroom

to pucker up with Vaseline. Won't poke the elephant.

Don't poke the elephant. The film's concluding: lights expose

our affected bodies, jittery, clammy, dry. But then

a kiss to end an unromantic film.

This is (and was) a sonnet, but some of the lines in the first version felt overlong. The shape on the page was not as compact as it might have been. If you check the second version you will notice the strength of the words at the end of most lines (they are mainly verbs or nouns) compared to those of the first version.

But just changing the line breaks to make the poem more compact in width, so to speak, would slide the lines down the page and result in a longer poem of about fifteen or sixteen lines. To keep the poem a sonnet one needs to edit carefully, plucking out words that are not necessary so the poem remains fourteen lines long.

The grade of '1st' is not about perfection but about the marker having confidence in the student writer. In the original poem the overall balance of sound and meaning, and the 'speakability' of the poem is excellent. There are sharp word choices: 'thought-out knees' are placed just so, close to the other person's knees but not touching; the 'elephant' that mustn't be poked is the elephant in the room: is this a date … will they kiss or not? The emotions are shown in a sensory fashion (the hummingbird patter in the heart, the clammy skin) and not stated directly. There is space for the reader to imagine the scene. I enjoyed the repetition of 'side effects' and 'the elephant' (anaphora was a technique we'd tried out in a workshop). There is lots going on yet the poem feels effortlessly simple and direct.

The same story content might have been expressed as below, but this does not have the powerful language of the original poem, nor the formal qualities of the second version.

'Side Effects' (3)

I went to the cinema on a first date.

I was nervous. I sat down carefully so our knees did not touch.

I didn't know if we would kiss or not,

or who would make the first move.

So I tried to busy myself eating popcorn but spilt it in our laps.

I went to the bathroom to reapply Vaseline

and recover my cool. I came back out.

The lights came up and then he kissed me.

I quite like this but you can imagine it as prose, can't you? In its favour the line breaks are in good places: the two longest lines have the word 'touch' at the end and the spilling of popcorn 'in our laps'. By drawing the eye to these lines the poem gives the reader a summing-up of the longing and the awkwardness of the date. But both extended lines might have been broken and placed below their current positions. This would *still* have drawn the eye as they would have become the shortest lines in the poem.

The rush of the last line still works well: it feels like defeat ('the lights came up') but turns into something else ('and then he kissed me'). To the poem's detriment, the word choices are not very imaginative and the images created are nowhere near as strong as the ones in the original version of this poem. This is an average sort of poem and the overall mark would depend on the quality of the neighbouring poems. At Level 6 this is probably a 52–4.

Now let us return to the ape and his (or her) fleas.

Task Completion – What did you write?

If you came up with 'The apes yawn and *scratch* their fleas in the sun' you've chosen a predictable verb, and if the rest of the poem was like this, then the feedback comments might be 'prosaic' (that is, sounds like prose) or 'weak word choices'. This is going to get an average 54–8 mark.

'The apes yawn and *flick* their fleas in the sun' or 'The apes yawn and *pick* their fleas in the sun' are both better choices. The verb is more visual, delicate and engaging. It brings into focus the ape's hands that hopefully will be seen again. Feedback comments might be 'satisfying word choices'. This is more like a 60 plus.

'The apes yawn and *adore* their fleas in the sun' is striking, almost peculiar, but highly visual: the ape picks off a flea, stares at it with a careful concentration. Excellent. This type of writing is of 1st quality. It is also the verb that Ted Hughes used in his poem, 'The Jaguar'.

Observe how the experts make their decisions and then return to your own poems. Do remember a strong word choice does not mean using fancy or excessive words. Hughes did not say, 'The apes yawn elegantly and adore their basalt fleas in the molten-lava sun.' That would be too much. Incidentally, the next line is, 'The parrots shriek as if they were on fire', and so the poem continues to startle the reader.

After astonishing word choices, the most notable quality in excellent poems is a playful sense of rhythm. This does not mean an endless 'de-dum, de-dum, de-dum, de-dum, de-dum' drum beat with no variation. You *could* tap your finger gently to a poem and find that strong syllable sounds land on the beat, but *some* of the phrases in a satisfying poem will probably trickle across the beat. Beats are very hard to describe without speaking out loud and tapping a table, so I won't spend long on this. I would draw your attention to how the first and second versions of 'Side Effects' end. Version one has lines in the sextet (the last six lines of a sonnet) that run: 7, 9, 9, 7, 5, 5 beats. The second version (my version) goes 7, 7, 7, 7, 7, 5 beats. The new edit creates not only greater visual coherence on the page but sets up an expectation of a pattern (the 7 beats) so that the alteration of the pattern is an enjoyable surprise.

I would suggest if rhythm is causing you problems then ask your tutor for a tutorial on rhythm. What you want to create is *poems that feel like they are written for adults,* and not nursery rhymes. Rhythm is fluid and should be heard rather than seen. I would recommend you read your work out loud before your final edit, if you do not already do so.

Finally, try comparing the last two lines of the poems out loud. Even though the words are practically the same you should find that in the second version this revised arrangement *pushes* the penultimate line a little further so that the rush of the shorter final line makes that kiss more felt.

Small things, but small things matter in a poem.

Dissertation or Final Portfolio

The more you read (books, magazines, online) and hear (radio or performance) and view (stage or film) the more you will be able to identify what is weak, or good, or really great writing. By your third year you will have an idea of what suits you and hopefully you can focus upon this in your final portfolio submission. In a longer submission at Level 6 you may now be giving more consideration to the quantity of work you have produced and how best to arrange it.

Quantity of writing

Ideally you will have created more work than you need. Where this is the case, line up what you feel is your best work and also your more diverse work. If the portfolio is long enough it is probably a good idea to show prose that is written in the first person *and also* a piece in the third person; work that has sensory description, some short passages of exposition *but also* lively scenes with dialogue. What I would avoid is one piece that takes up your entire word count and is restricted to one main technique. Unless you have a brilliant style, hedging your bets and covering several styles of writing is probably a good idea for most students.

A 4,000-word story that seems flat because each event is tagged together as 'and then this happened and then that happened and then this happened' might well get a lower mark than one story of 1,000 words in this style placed with two others of 1,500 words that offer dramatic scenes and/or dialogue. This is not to say that an expository style can never be done well (there are whole novels that use it), but remember you are putting all your eggs in one basket if you make one long short story the entirety of your submission.

The exception to this is if the dissertation module has already insisted that your submission be one continuous piece of writing, such as work from a novel. If this is the case it could be a good idea to present the opening and closing chapters and something from the middle. It is also common to present the opening three chapters. You need not have written the entire book, but try and apply yourself to these areas. This will show your marker that you can create a clear structure for your work and handle openings and endings.

With poetry you might want to consider including some poems that are utterly free verse, some that are slightly more structured free verse and some that are strict form. Arguably, some poets say there is no such thing as 'utterly free' verse because once you put words on the page there is some kind of presentation going on – thus structure. But you need to recognize how and why you are making your structural editing decisions. If your portfolio suggests a maximum line count (e.g., 120 lines), it might not be the best idea to do this as one long poem. Again, like the prose submission, it becomes a case of all your eggs in one basket. But do check with your tutor. It might be that your long poem *is* your best work.

Bear in mind that choosing to spread variety in theme and format across your submission will also give you more to write about if you have to write an accompanying critical essay. However, for higher achieving students you might already know where your strengths and focus lies. Pursuing one theme or small group of techniques might be your best ploy. If you are presenting a mixed portfolio (poems *and* prose *and* script) I would be inclined to present work that has parallels in theme since the differing forms may otherwise be distracting. The marker should not feel that you are randomly trying out everything! That may have been acceptable in the first year ('experimenting'), and possibly in the second, but in your final year, if you have the option of a free portfolio, try to make it feel coherent.

Ordering your work

Start and finish well, and leave them wanting more! That is, put your strongest work at the beginning and end, and consider going under the word count rather than over it. The person marking your work is marking a very big pile of portfolios and although you will probably have an allowance of 10 per cent either way (e.g., 3,600–4,400 on a 4,000-word portfolio), the tutor marking twenty portfolios of 4,000 words will be marking considerably more if all those students submit the maximum 4,400 words. Utilizing the 10 per cent leeway on the word count would not affect your final mark outcome, but should give you pause for thought: are you *really* convinced that what your stories have to say could not be said in 4,000 words or fewer? Often the longer portfolio has the effect of suggesting to a marker that the student ran out of time to redraft, and didn't edit it as well as he or she might have done.

Having decided upon the first and last piece in your portfolio you will need to consider how to arrange the remaining pieces of work. One choice is to order the stories or poems so that they pursue an emotional thread from, say, dark and dramatic to light and humorous. Your other choice is to place contrasting material side by side. Rather than create an evolving emotional theme you instead aim to surprise the reader with opposing views or themes. The risk with this second approach is that the reader/marker will find themselves reading a poem about someone's death followed by a slapstick kind of poem. You probably don't want to jolt the reader too much, but contrasts can sometimes work (e.g., a sad story about war followed by a satirical poem about money), especially if there is a tenuous link that the reader can add for themselves.

The choice of arrangement is up to you and learning how to do it to suit the work you produce is part of becoming more professional as a writer. If you have read a number of poetry collections or short story collections by now and found favourites, you could re-read these with a particular focus on how they have been arranged. You can do this with a short story collection by just re-reading the opening and closing paragraphs of each story to remind you of the story's plot and the tone. *Then* see how that writer (or the editor if it is an anthology) has decided to order the material. Arguably an anthology is attempting to be 'dip in and out–able' whereas a single-author collection wants to sustain a more linear interest. Certainly poems will want to 'speak to one another' across a collection. A script will most likely be entirely self-contained and function as one short story (or possibly two: plot and subplot). Make sure you follow each narrative arc through and pay close attention to the beginnings and ends.

Make use of your tutor. Ideally go to a tutorial with a selection of work and ask their advice on which might be your strongest pieces, or which might work together. Tutors can best advise you when you come with specific questions and concrete pieces of work to discuss, not just a set of an ideas of what you *might* be writing.

It is an often-repeated piece of advice (and does not fit *every* example of good writing, but does fit much contemporary writing): if you can read your work out loud without any glitches and bumps then you may have achieved a good fluent style. This is especially true for lyric poetry, and if that is the style your university department favours, then get comfortable with using your spoken voice to help edit and refine your written words.

Titles

Think about your titles. Titles are a small but important thing. *The Great Gatsby* was originally called *Trimalchio in West Egg*. Yikes! The poem I quoted earlier, 'The Jaguar', is self-explanatory, but sometimes you can get something extra from a title. 'Pearl & Dean' was an excellent title choice for a student's short story that explored the relationship between two characters who met in the 1940s and loved going to the cinema. The title refers to both the names of the lead characters *and* the cinematic advertising giant.

If you can, try and create titles that 'add something extra' or create hints for your story, script or poem. You will probably think of the title after you have written the piece, but that is quite normal so don't become stressed about it. However, do remember that titled work is always preferable to work that comes in with 'Untitled' on it. If you're really stuck, use a time or season (*High Noon, 3:10 to Yuma, This September Sun*), a place (*Little Gidding* or *Cold Mountain*) or your character's name (*Carrie, Peter Pan*), or any combination of name, place and job (*Colonel Barker's Blackpool Posting*). You might also use a popular expression (*One for the Money*), or maybe a saying with a twist (*Live and Let Die*), but try not to be too clichéd.

Another cheeky possibility that can work, for a poem in particular, is to give a simple but atmospheric piece a title that suggests more depth – for example, for a poem about the sky, 'The Day You Disappeared'. But if you do that, make sure there are no lingering lines about missing his/her face, etc. as that would push it towards the over-obvious. Allow the reader to make the connections.

In the 'real world' an intriguing title can encourage an agent to read the rest of your submitted work, or encourage a reader in a bookshop to pick up your book. So don't neglect to think of one.

> Make a record of any articles about writing craft, passages in literature or flyers from performances that inspired you, that will then help you be objectively critical when you come to writing reflective commentaries about your writing journey.
>
> (Jen, Year Two, BA Creative Writing)

> I found two other students whose work I liked and we swapped work in the second and third year. It really helped to get extra feedback and to keep me motivated.
>
> (Mark, Year Three, BA Creative Writing)

Marketing

Creative writing courses may include elements of marketing within their taught programmes, but for some marketing is a course for MA students, or outside the scope of university teaching. We are all aware that certain non-literary works can achieve blockbuster sales figures from marketing campaigns, word-of-mouth hype or social media 'buzz', but had such work been submitted for a degree course the author might only have achieved a 3rd! Sex and suspense sells – given the right marketing or the right 'moment'. But tutors do not want to encourage poor writing even if a student has a talent for hype, or a rapport with the zeitgeist. Sometimes bad but timely work will get published and may also sell, but we prefer to focus our teaching on literary craft and communication techniques that are also transferable skills.

Many publishers may now expect you to have an active social media network and to be prepared to promote your own books, as their own budgets for marketing may be tiny. For poets this means doing plenty of live gigs and touring. For novelists your online presence and activity within others' blogs and book review sites may be important.

The prevalence of online media reviews and 'sharing', from Amazon reviews to Facebook to specialized websites, might make you want to reconsider your current online presence and how much of yourself you wish to reveal. It is not only privacy that is an issue but the overall tone you use for your Facebook updates or blog entries. Are you generous and helpful? Or cynical? Readers or followers will judge you on your tone of 'voice' as well as your content. I am not suggesting you should create a false online presence, but perhaps consider putting your best self forward.

In addition it is important to realize that even with a large 'following' on a blog or Twitter account this may not translate into book sales. Followers will prefer free content over purchased content, and positive feedback on a blog, though encouraging, may not result in direct sales. Overconfidence is not a good idea. But certainly include information about your social media presence in your sales pitch to potential agents and publishers.

Work Placements

Placements are sometimes arranged for degree students in their second or third years to give the student some real-life experience in literary events, festival management, publishing or some other field. They are usually for a specific time period and there will be a set-up meeting with student, tutor and organization representative, a midway meeting and then an end meeting. Usually the student will be left on their own with the organization for the rest of the time period. The student's report will probably be the method of assessment, together with a report (verbal at the final meeting, or possibly written) given by the organization's representative.

Placement at a library or reading group

Prior to my becoming a university lecturer I ran a community poetry organization. I coordinated open floors, guest nights, workshops, training, various short-term projects and two library-based reading groups. On one occasion we had a student on placement work with us. On the whole her contributions were helpful but one sequence of events might serve as a useful learning exercise.

The student on placement was attending one of our daytime reading groups to observe the group facilitator in action. The group comprised mainly elderly readers who did not come to our other evening-based activities. We were proud to have involved members of the community who were not otherwise engaging with community poetry events.

Part way through the placement the facilitator of the reading group came to me to say she was confused by something that had occurred. The student on placement had issued the entire group with a form to fill in. The form asked the group's members about their experiences of the group and also gathered some information on equal opportunities. Some of the group had been disconcerted by questions 'about their personal lives', as they put it. The facilitator thought I had issued these forms to the student to distribute! I was shocked: both by the fact that the forms had gone out without the student having thought to check with me, and also because I felt the group might lose trust in us. I was concerned that when the time came for us to issue our own review forms (as most organizations do from time to time as part of their pledge with funders) the group might be reluctant to complete them.

Of course, I had to raise this with the student and her tutor, and the student was embarrassed and apologetic: she simply had not thought there would be a problem. But what students on placement should always remember is that groups or audiences or individuals that are accessible to you *because of the placement* are not 'yours' in any way. However, you will be seen as representing the placement organization. How you act may have repercussions for the organization (rather than, say, for your university, though that is also a possibility).

If you want to gather information about a group or audience for a university assessment exercise you *must* check this with the organization first. If this is authorized then you need to be clear with the group that you are gathering the information *for your own purposes as a student and not for the organization*. This is a matter of responsibility and ethics: people need to know where their private information or opinions might be taken. Also, if you take information at an inappropriate moment, it may be difficult for the organization to gather information for themselves in the future. Be cautious.

General advice

Be clear about what you need to do to fulfil the objectives of the placement from the university's point of view and be clear about what the placement organization itself expects you to do.

Know what the final assessment/write-up will be and give yourself enough time for it. Put all meeting dates in your diary!

Keep a journal even if the university don't require you to: this will enable you to check exactly what you did and when. On writing this up as a report you will be grateful to be reminded of things you may have forgotten doing.

Boundaries 1: Do not initiate anything with the client group / general public without checking with the work placement if that's OK.

Boundaries 2: If the work placement organization ask you to do anything that makes you feel uncomfortable, check with your university if it is necessary.

This includes late hours, solo working and perhaps handling money. The chances are your university will have already checked all this out, but be aware that you can say 'no', or you can ask for time to 'check with my tutor' or to 'check my timetable' to stall making a decision.

Boundaries 3: Don't expect the placement workers to be your friends even if you feel you have lots in common. They are doing a job, they have limited funds, they are probably anxious about numerous things that they won't share with you. Keep within your boundaries. For example, if they give you a mobile phone number to stay in touch during an event you are helping to organize, *don't* share this number with others without permission, and don't start adding them to your group texts about your social life!

And the obvious: Be polite and be on time. Don't ask them to read your novel! If they are agents or publishers follow the usual procedures. Perhaps let them know that *after* the placement you intend to send them a sample of your work.

> I'd have checked out public transport and done a 'dry run' to my work placement *before* the placement started. I was late first day. Rookie error.
>
> (Lee, Year Three, BA Creative Writing)

> I worked really hard and kept copies of everything. I loved my placement (once I got over the embarrassment of being late that first day).
>
> (Elizabeth, Year Three, BA Creative Writing)

Continuing Writing and Professional Opportunities

What can I do after I graduate? you might ask. What further opportunities are there for writers? The final part of this chapter comprises two sections: Further Study and Professional Opportunities. A great deal has changed and continues to change in the world of publishing. The *Writers' and Artists' Yearbook* may keep you up to date on this with chapters about digital changes and e-publishing. Your university may also offer a module in professional development; certainly some MA courses do. In the meantime consider the information below.

Further study: MAs and PhDs

If you're thinking about further study at university you will need to consider cost and also where you might study. Cost might lead you to study close to home, but if you have the freedom to roam then make sure you assess all the aspects of each course. Some MAs are modular and some are much more workshop driven with little assessment except for the final portfolio and accompanying critical essay. Modular learning might allow you to spread your interests wider, or take up new ones – children's fiction, for example. You might also want an MA that offers something extra, such as professional development. An MA course in Critical and Creative Writing or Writing and Teaching Creative Writing may sound more appealing than plain creative writing, so examine as many options as you can. You could try distance learning – often such courses are cheaper than campus-based courses and more compatible with holding down a day job.

If you think you might want to move on from an MA to a PhD then pay close attention to who the course lecturers are – and read their books. You will want to work with someone you admire. If you find that you end up doing an MA in one place and then need to attend interviews, change universities or move house for your PhD, there will be additional costs to you. Of course, your interests might change between MA and PhD which is fine, but a bit of research before the MA might save you some money.

In terms of funding, do watch the jobs.ac.uk website from January. This is when universities start posting information about funded PhDs. There have been recent ones in specific areas such as Black British Poetry in Performance, and open AHRC-funded PhDs, at different universities from Scotland down to Plymouth. An AHRC place will pay your fees and then give you around £8,000 a year to live on. Some universities also offer teaching bursaries: on my PhD my fees were paid by teaching undergraduates for one workshop per week; I was also offered some additional teaching which helped me avoid debt.

Bear in mind that further study will improve your current level of writing but it will *not* guarantee publication and it will *not* guarantee a teaching job at university. Whilst creative writing may be an expanding area of interest for students, universities are quite cautious about employing tutors because of the uncertain state of play with the high fee levels now in place.

Postgraduate study can be a tricky matter to deal with on your CV. Some employers will be concerned about employing someone whom they see as 'overqualified', so it is a good idea to keep working if you can, and create several CVs for the purposes of differing kinds of employment. Thus additional years of study can be covered by the years you spent working in a part-time job (e.g., in a retail environment or café). That said, I enjoyed my PhD and I am glad

I did it, so if you really want to do one, have worked out a way to pay for it, and have been offered a place, then good luck.

Our tutorials were optional so I didn't go in my first year. But they're really helpful. If you're nervous about seeing a tutor on your own you could ask if two of you could go together because you have the same questions. (Tutors like this 'cos it saves time). I did that in my second year and it made me more confident to go alone in my third year.

(Misha, Year Three, BA Creative Writing)

Professional opportunities and resources

For script

Your local theatre, festival or 'fringe' scene may have new writing schemes. Be aware that some groups are funded for the 16–25s, so get in there whilst you're young enough! All theatres now have web presences and that might be the best way to find out about new writing showcase events – for example, Birmingham's Drum theatre, Leeds's West Yorkshire Playhouse, Manchester's Royal Exchange and the Contact Theatre (local community / black and, separately, queer remits), Liverpool's Everyman and Playhouse, Cardiff's Theatre Cymru – and that's not mentioning those in London (who get most of the press coverage): the Royal Court, the National and many others.

Attend performances and then look up the theatre company involved online – most companies tour and are not embedded in a theatre building. Join their e-news mailing list. Some will put out calls for new work.

The BBC Writersroom (www.bbc.co.uk/writersroom) lists a broad range of opportunities and also has interviews with writers. There's a script archive too, so you can read episodes from TV and radio drama and occasionally feature-length dramas (TV films).

There is also a *Screenwriter's Handbook* rather like the *Writers' and Artists' Yearbook* – not a 'how to write screenplays' but a 'where to send them' type of book. Don't rule out DIY film and YouTube exposure.

For poetry

The route to publication for a poet is generally: magazines, a pamphlet and then a collection. Agents do not work for poets except where they are already famous, tour a great deal (John Hegley) or possibly work across forms (Simon

Armitage writes poetry, novels and plays, so does Sophie Hannah). Touring is also a possibility (Kate Tempest and George the Poet tour, do summer festivals, and have appeared on Channel 4's *Random Acts* slots). Join an organization like Apples and Snakes and learn to do gigs and workshops in schools. Or get to know your local Arts Council of England (www.artscouncil.org.uk) regional literature officer and apply for small project funding.

Poetry magazines are often more credible than some competitions – and have the bonus of only costing you the postage involved to submit work and not a fee. (If it's a submission by e-mail, then that's at no cost!) Most magazines won't pay you but will send you a free copy of the magazine once published. A few do pay, such as *Poetry London*, the *Rialto* and *Poetry Wales*. Magazine publication gives you the credibility to approach a publisher. Don't approach a publisher without some track record in magazines, as publishers are inundated with wannabe poets' manuscripts and probably won't read past your cover letter.

The poetry library in London has a great online presence and lists competitions, magazines and publishers. The competitions are only shown for the current and forthcoming month – but be reassured there are competitions throughout the year. The larger and better known will usually cost more to enter. Do be wise about how much you can afford to spend on competitions as you might be sending work out every month. There is also a poetry library in Scotland.

The Poetry Society in London publish the magazine *Poetry Review*, run events and have a very diverse website. Some university libraries subscribe to *Poetry Review* so you can read it without having to spend any money yourself.

The Poetry Book Society offers selected books for its membership fee and a newsletter. It offers free student membership They run competitions that are open only to members and they host the T. S. Eliot Awards each year.

The Poetry Archive (www.poetryarchive.org) has recordings by a huge number of published poets (alongside the poem's text). It links over to the American site, the Poetry Foundation, for American poets. You can also perform searches for things such as strict form.

For prose

The route to publication is usually: short story publication in magazines to build a profile and gain experience and contacts; acquire an agent with a first novel; get a publisher. After the success of a novel you might be asked to do a short story collection (as with Jennifer Egan). Occasionally an author might have a short story collection out first, but usually this is through a competition with publication offered as a prize; mainstream publishers don't see short stories as commercial.

Thresholds is a short story forum run by the University of Chichester. Look out for links to National Short Story Day, etc. (blogs.chi.ac.uk/shortstoryforum).

The final pages in Ailsa Cox's *Writing Short Stories* (2005) lists dozens of magazines in print and online that publish short stories (and in some cases poems too).

Short story publishers who publish anthologies and single-author collections include Unthank Books and Comma Press. Nightjar Press do a chapbook/ pamphlet publication for one long short story. Also, consider Salt's anthologies of short stories as they pick out previously published stories to form a 'best of the year' selection. This means when you look in the index you would see where the story was first published (e.g., other short story publishers such as *Granta* and *Strand* magazines).

For everyone

Writers' and Artists' Yearbook: Reference copies exist in city centre libraries as well as university libraries. It contains essays by famous writers in different fields. It covers journalism and illustration as well as creative writing, and lists agents and publishers.

Ideastap.com: If you create a profile you can log into all that Ideas Tap offers. There are plenty of student- and ex-student-related materials such as articles on internships, job applications, becoming an independent artist or self-employed, etc. But they also arrange regular competitions (free to enter) and promote training events in everything from performance poetry to children's theatre to photography. Their jobs and opportunities tab is a very good one with nationwide opportunities.

Mslexia magazine: (www.mslexia.co.uk) is aimed at women writers but is available online as well as in print and can be read by anyone. Useful articles, interviews, exercises, competitions (poetry, poetry pamphlet, debut novel, children's/YA novel).

Wasafiri magazine: black and minority ethnic writing from black and white writers. Interviews, articles, conferences, and also new writing. Copies are expensive but if you search the backlist you might find something invaluable to you (e.g., a special issue on children's fiction). Some university libraries subscribe.

DaDaFest in Liverpool host an annual festival of disability-focused arts, writing and drama activities with some terrific guests. Graeae Theatre specialize in disability-led theatre and some of their plays have been published by Methuen. *Disability Arts* covers all art forms and is available online. There are a few magazines that specialize in mental health issues / survivors' writing (www.survivorspoetry.org). The *Lumen* at Edinburgh University is interested in health/illness writing. There is an academic *Journal of Literary and Cultural Disability Studies* based at Liverpool Hope University. *Poets Against ATOS* is an online publication and publishes a wide variety of poetry. The Hippocrates Prize is a poetry award for writing related to medicine and has categories for NHS staff, one for young writers and one that is open.

LGBT(QIA) material will suit many publications, but one that specializes is the US journal *Adrienne* (for queer women) from Sibling Rivalry Press (online). The press also has a couple of magazines for men (for poets and for short story writers), and they publish occasional books.

A final brilliant resource is your library. City centre libraries are often larger than local branches and may host reading groups or writing groups. Continue to use the library after you've finished university: freely loaned books are a wonder and a gift. In particular it is a good way to become familiar with a new genre without spending lots of money – exploring, say, children's fiction or graphic novels. Look out for free giveaway book offers on World Book Day.

> The university magazine society is the best place to go to find opportunities for aspiring or experienced writers. [Your city may have / My city had] loads of brilliant monthly poetry nights and writing groups. The atmosphere at indie poetry nights is always supportive and encouraging, and simply having the confidence to get up on stage and perform is a great boost to your writing, as well as you get to meet lots of like-minded people. Be brave!
>
> (Emma, Year Three, BA Creative Writing)

We hope you've enjoyed, or will enjoy, the final year of your degree. You'll have learned a lot about yourself and your abilities as a writer. We hope these chapters were useful and helped in this discovery. Most of all we wish you well in whatever path you choose to pursue.

BIBLIOGRAPHY

Year One and Year Two: Prose

Alternative, non-academic thinking about writing:
Atwood, M. 1988. *A Handmaid's Tale*. Boston: Houghton Mifflin.
Brande, D. 1981. *Becoming a Writer*. Los Angeles: Tarcher.
Cameron, J. 2012. *The Artist's Way*. London: Souvenir.

Cox, A. 2007. *Writing Short Stories*. London: Routledge.
Franzen, J. 2000. *How to Be Alone*. London: Fourth Estate.
Goldberg, N. 2005. *Writing Down the Bones*. Boston: Shambhala.
Graham, R., et al. 2013. *The Road to Somewhere*. London: Palgrave Macmillan.
Iser, W. 1980. *The Act of Reading*. Maryland: Johns Hopkins University Press.
Lodge, D. 2012. *The Art of Fiction*. London: Vintage Digital.
May, S., and H. Blakemore. 2008. *Creative Writing Subject Benchmark Statement*. York: NAWE.
Rimmon-Kenan, S. 2002. *Narrative Fiction: Contemporary Poetics*. London: Routledge.

Journals

Short Fiction in Theory and Practice (Edge Hill University). Online: http://www.intellectbooks.co.uk/journals/view-issue,id=1950 (accessed 8 May 2014).
Short Fiction Journal (Plymouth University). Online: http://www.shortfictionjournal.co.uk (accessed 8 May 2014).

Websites

East of the Web: http://www.eastoftheweb.com (accessed 8 May 2014).

NAWE (National Association of Writers in Education): http://www.nawe.co.uk (accessed 8 May 2014).

NetGalley: https://www.netgalley.com (accessed 8 May 2014).

The *New Yorker*: http://www.newyorker.com (accessed 8 May 2014).

The *Short Review*: http://thenewshortreview.wordpress.com (accessed 8 May 2014).

The *White Review*: http://www.thewhitereview.org (accessed 8 May 2014).

Thresholds: http://blogs.chi.ac.uk/shortstoryforum (accessed 8 May 2014).

Year Three: Poetry and Script

Poetry advice

Herbert, W. N., and Matthew Hollis. 2000. *Strong Words: Modern Poets on Modern Poetry*. Tarset: Bloodaxe Books.

Lennard, John. 2005. *The Poetry Handbook: A Guide to Reading Poetry for Pleasure and Practical Criticism*. Oxford: Oxford University Press.

Oliver, Mary. 1994. *A Poetry Handbook*. San Diego/London: Harcourt.

Padel, Ruth. 2002. *52 Ways of Looking at a Poem*. London: Chatto & Windus.

_____. 2007. *The Poem and the Journey: 60 Poems for the Journey of Life*. London: Vintage.

Parini, Jay. 2008. *Why Poetry Matters*. New Haven: Caravan Books (Yale University).

Sweeney, Matthew, and John Hartley-Williams. 2010. *Write Poetry and Get It Published*. Teach Yourself. London: Hodder Headline.

Wainwright, Jeffrey. 2004. *Poetry: The Basics*. London: Routledge.

Poetry collections

Atkinson, Tiffany. 2006. *Kink and Particle*. Bridgend: Seren.

Miller, Kei. 2010. *A Light Song of Light*. Manchester: Carcanet.

Paterson, Don. 2004. *Landing Light*. London: Faber.

Swift, Todd, and Kim Lockwood, eds. 2012. *Lung Jazz: Young British Poets for Oxfam*. Gwynedd: Cinnamon Press.

Shapcott, Jo. 2006. *Her Book: Poems 1988–1998*. London: Faber.

Simmonds, Kathryn. 2008. *Sundays at the Skin Launderette*. Bridgend: Seren.

Symmons Roberts, Michael. 2004. *Corpus*. London: Cape.

Script advice

Boardman-Jacobs, Sam, ed. 2004. *Radio Scriptwriting*. Bridgend: Seren.

Edgar, David, 2009. *How Plays Work*. London: Nick Hern Books.

Field, Syd. 1984. *The Screenwriter's Workbook*. New York: Dell.

Gooch, Steve. 1995. *Writing a Play*. London: A & C Black.

Greig, Noel. 2005. *Playwriting: A Practical Guide*. New York: Routledge.

Longmore, Paul. 'Screening Stereotypes: Images of Disabled People in Television and Motion Pictures'. *Social Policy* (summer 1985): 31–3. (Also in Gartner, Alan, and Tom Joe, ed. 1986. *Images of the Disabled, Disabling Images*. Westport, CT: Greenwood Press.)

McWhinnie, Donald. 1959. *The Art of Radio*. London: Faber and Faber.

Mitchell, David T., and Sharon Snyder. 2000. *Narrative Prosthesis: Disability and the Dependencies of Discourse*. Michigan: University of Michigan. (This book examines how disability is represented in literature. Chapter 4 discusses portrayals of Richard III.)

Neipris, Janet. 2005. *To Be a Playwright*. New York/London: Routledge.

Shingler, Martin, and Cindy Weiringa. 1998. *On Air: Methods and Meanings of Radio*. London: Arnold.

Turner, Barry, ed. 2010. *The Screenwriter's Handbook*. Basingstoke: Palgrave Macmillan.

Some suggested scripts

Agbaje, Bola. 2007. *Gone Too Far!* London: Methuen Drama.

Beckett, Samuel. 1965. *All That Fall*. London: Faber and Faber.

(First broadcast on radio in 1957. First use of radiophonic – i.e., distorted/exaggerated – sound for expressionistic effect.)

_____. 1986. *Waiting for Godot*. London: Faber and Faber.

(First broadcast in France in French in 1952; first staged in 1953 in French; first staged in Britain in English in 1955.)

Churchill, Carol, 2003. *Far Away*. London: Nick Hern.

(Short play, future dystopian setting.)

Dear, Nick. 1989. *'The Art of Success' and 'In The Ruins': Two Plays*. London: Methuen.

(These plays show how to create historical-sounding but lively dialogue.)

Hall, Lee. 2000. *Spoonface Steinberg*. London: Methuen Drama.

(First broadcast in 1997. Sony Award–winning radio play, written as a monologue from an autistic child. You may know Hall for *Billy Elliot*. He also wrote the screenplay for *War Horse*.)

Neilson, Anthony. 2007. '*The Wonderful World of Dissocia*' and '*Realism*'. London: Methuen

(Drama. Young playwright. *Realism* is surreal and takes place in the protagonist's head.)

Sealey, Jenny. 2002. *Graeae Plays 1: New Plays Redefining Disability*. London: Aurora Metro.

(Six plays written by playwrights with disabilities who challenge the assumption that disability theatre is either 'worthy' or appealing to the sympathy of its audiences. Includes *Fittings: The Last Freakshow* and *Peeling*.)

Taylor, Ali. 2008. *Overspill*. London: Nick Hern Books.

(A poetic play about three friends who are together when a bomb goes off in London.)

CONCLUSION

There will be a moment, not too long from when you first purchased this guide, that you will be sat in a darkened theatre in an uncomfortable gown that keeps slipping off your shoulders to reveal the smart new outfit you bought specially for today. You'll be surrounded by your peers, muttering about destinations, the summer and how long does this need to take, really? Your breathing is shallow, your hands clammy and sore from clapping, your hair looks ridiculous (maybe). You're waiting for your name to be called. They're only on the As! Your gran's been taking pictures of everyone that goes on stage – *because she wouldn't want to miss you, would she?* And then … they call your name. Doesn't matter that your gran's ran out of space on the camera, or that your hair's sticking up at the back like a flustered cockatiel, take your time getting to the stage, smile and celebrate your achievement. Yes it's the end of your degree, but it's absolutely the beginning of your future.

We hope this guide helps see you through those years of hard work, discovery and inspiration. Whatever degree programme or combination of English literature, language and creative writing you undertake, you will develop a greater understanding of the world around you, how it is constructed and our place within it. You'll be able to articulate your own critical, and in some cases creative, responses and observations of that world in a more thoughtful, academic and energetic manner than when you started. The skills you learn will be valuable in both your personal lives and your careers. This prolonged and focused study changes you for good.

The authors would like to thank all of the students, past and present, for being so kind as to donate their time, thoughts and work. This guide has been written in response to their experiences in the hope that it will help future students do what they have done and are doing: to pass their degree.

Shh – wait, is that your name they're calling?

Sarah Dobbs, February 2014

INDEX

Lightning Source UK Ltd.
Milton Keynes UK
UKOW03f0256200914

238891UK00001B/12/P

9 781783 082889